NAFSA's Guide to

International Student Recruitment

2nd Edition

NAFSA

Association of
International Educators
Washington, D.C.

Edited by
Linda Heaney

NAFSA: Association of International Educators is a member organization promoting international education and providing professional development opportunities to the field. Hundreds of NAFSA members volunteer to serve the Association and thousands advocate for international education. NAFSA serves international educators and their institutions and organizations by setting standards of good practice, providing training and professional development opportunities, providing networking opportunities, and advocating for international education.

For more information about NAFSA, visit www.nafsa.org

International Standard Book Number: 0-912207-93-0

Library of Congress Cataloging-in-Publication Data

NAFSA's guide to international student recruitment / edited by Linda Heaney. -- 2nd ed.
    p. cm.

Includes bibliographical references and index.
    ISBN 978-0-912207-93-3 (pbk.)
    1. Students, Foreign--Recruiting--United States. 2. College students--Recruiting--United States. I. Heaney, Linda. II. Title: Guide to international student recruitment.

LB2342.82.N24 2009
378.1'982691--dc22

                                                                    2009014730

Edited by Jan Steiner, NAFSA
Cover Design and production by Cheryl D. Collins, NAFSA

Printed in the United States

Contents

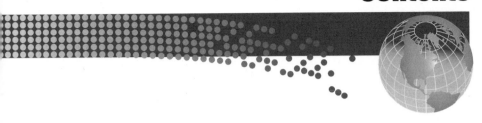

Contents (continued)

Acknowledgments

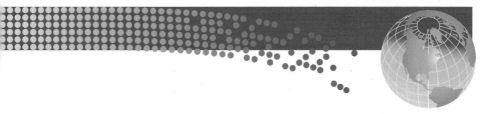

Gathering 23 NAFSA members together to share their experience and expertise, in written form, is both a challenge and a pleasure. The challenge arises from the fact that these are busy people with full-time jobs and personal lives; the pleasure comes from watching them translate their knowledge into words with such ease and generosity. These are the best and most experienced NAFSAns in their field, and it has been my joy to collaborate with them on this book.

The book also owes much to Christopher Murphy who can guide a tanker through a small tree-strewn stream and Jan Steiner whose editing skills are only surpassed by her sense of humor and desire to produce a first-rate publication. Kate Trayte Freeman and John Eriksen, members par excellence, provided guidance and encouragement every step of the way. It's always a positive, joyful, and educational experience when one works with such professionals.

I would be remiss if I did not acknowledge the fine work by editors Marie O'Hara, Karen Raftus, and Joann Stedman and the authors of the first edition of *NAFSA's Guide to International Recruitment* published in 1999. They crafted a solid foundation upon which to build, and it was enlightening to see just how much the field has developed and grown.

Finally, I want to thank all of the members of NAFSA who have presented at conferences and workshops, served on committees, and held leadership positions in the area of international admissions. They have worked consistently over many years to set the bar high, establish best practices, and share their expertise with their colleagues so that students could leave their home country and pursue higher education abroad.

Linda Heaney
March 2009

Introduction

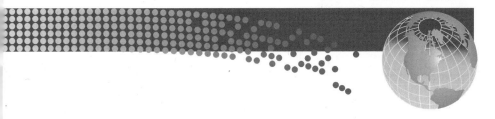

Marketing U.S. Higher Education in the Global Landscape

Linda Heaney

Though the writers of each chapter wrote from their own frame of reference, that of a U.S. institution, the information they have presented is no less meaningful or useful for institutions around the world.

After nearly a decade of faltering and sputtering, U.S. universities are again attracting to their campuses the best and brightest students from around the world. They have weathered the post-September 11 crises of new visa procedures and an environment of suspicion and have come to recognize that international students bring talent, income, and diversity to their institution, community, and region. Global trends have worked in their favor in recent years while competition from other countries has forced university officials to be more proactive in their recruitment efforts. As a result, U.S. colleges and universities, with some assistance from the U.S. government, have created programs, harnessed resources, and channeled their energies into showcasing their institutions while increasing applications and enrollments. The same is true for many other countries, such as Canada, Australia, and Qatar. Today's economic storm clouds are sure to produce some course changes, but the proverbial "recruitment ship" has righted itself and is sailing easier with the prevailing winds.

A snapshot of the last decade shows the dip in international students studying in the United States in 1998 as a result of the Asian currency crisis, followed by a slight uptick before the tragic events of 9/11. Since those days enrollment has been on a long slow rise to the fall of 2007 record of 623,805 international students, a 7 percent increase over the previous year (IIE 2008). A close look at the differences between 2000 and 2007 enrollments shows a gradual shift in academic level from 48 percent undergraduate and 45 percent graduate in 2000, to a 43 percent undergraduate and 49 percent graduate split in 2007, with the remainder enrolled in nondegree programs. While nine of the top ten sending countries remain the same, India, China, and South Korea now account for nearly 40 percent of the total U.S. international enrollment whereas students from these countries were 29 percent of the total in 2000 (IIE 2008).

Much of the increased attention to international students comes from the approximately $15.5 billion dollars they contribute to the U.S. economy through their tuition and living expenses, thus making U.S. higher education the country's fifth largest service sector export. Other countries have also increasingly understood this economic benefit. In a globalized world where business is about "competing with everyone from everywhere for everything," (Sirkin, Hemerling, and Bhattacharya 2008) political leaders and local business people have added their voices in support of international education. They have shared their networks, opened their pocket books, spoken forthrightly, and offered community support for international efforts. Many states, such as Indiana, Iowa, California, and Massachusetts, have created outreach programs for institutions in their states to tell their stories overseas. These cooperative ventures highlight the interdependence of universities, businesses, and government actions in today's world.

While tuition revenue is important to universities, the true competition is for talent. Universities seek the best students regardless of whether they are from Kentucky, Kazakhstan, or Korea. *The Economist* calls it "the battle for brainpower," and states that "the old battles for natural resources are being supplemented by new ones for talent."(Wooldridge 2006) The ability to solve complex problems, invent new solutions, and manage operations in different countries and time-zones with culturally diverse workforces are the tools of the twenty-first century; and these needs can only be met by a population with a university education. Thus, universities are now intent on identifying, attracting, enrolling, educating, and graduating bright and articulate young men and women.

In the worldwide search for talented, tuition-paying students, universities have a new ally in their own government. As nations decrease their own funding to universities, they now organize events, brand their country's educational institutions, and act as cheerleader for their universities in their recruitment efforts. Germany and Japan face declining and aging populations, so both governments have set goals for increasing international student enrollments. Jordan and Singapore see themselves as regional hubs for business, investment, and talent so they have announced targets of 150,000 by 2015 and 100,000 foreign students by 2020, respectively. Canada, Denmark, New Zealand, and the Netherlands now brand and market their institutions with slogans such as "Study in Holland: Open to International Minds" and "New Zealand Educated." (West 2008)

At the same time, young people are eager to take advantage of university offerings around the world. They yearn to increase their knowledge, expand their horizons, and create personal networks so they are marketable to future employers. The Organisation for Economic Co-operation and Development (OECD) estimated that in 2008 more than 2.9 million students were being educated at the tertiary level in countries other than their home country, up 58 percent from an estimated 1.7 million in 2000 (OECD 2008, 349), while a report from Australia estimates that the global demand for international higher education will grow to 3.72 million by 2025 (Banks, Olsen, and Pearce 2007).

What one sees early in the twenty-first century is a flirtatious dance by young people seeking adventure and the best preparation for their future, universities seeking good students and revenue, and regions and nations supporting their institutions so they have sustainable growth, investment opportunities, and jobs for their citizens. This fast-paced, multifaceted dance includes privately organized education fairs across the globe, university programs taught in English in non-English-speaking countries, aggressive advertising campaigns by countries that formerly restricted enrollments to their own citizens, the Bologna Declaration that eases academic movement for students and offers comparable courses and degrees for students in 29 European Union member states, and educational destinations such as Dubai Knowledge City, which boasts 350 institutional partners, and Education City Doha, home to six well-known U.S. universities.

According to *Project Atlas,* 20 percent of the world's mobile students are currently studying in the United States, 13 percent in the United Kingdom, 8 percent in France, 8 percent in Germany, 7 percent in China, and 7 percent in Australia (IIE 2008) These statistics reflect a 4 percent drop in U.S. market share since 2000.

While some in the United States express concern about the U.S. share of the market, past experience and recent trends together suggest that the United States can maintain its lead in attracting the largest share and the greatest number of international students. There are many reasons for the U.S. historical lead in international enrollments, recent changes that helped spark the rise in enrollments, and points to take into consideration when looking toward the future.

Historical Reasons

Quality: eight of ten and more than half of the top ten universities in the world are in the United States (Center for World-Class Universities 2008).

Quantity: 2,461 accredited four-year colleges and universities and 1,700 two-year colleges offer more than 500 programs of study to a total of 11 million students, clearly something for everyone.

Spending per student: the United States spends $24,370 per student, the highest in the world, and more than twice as much as the typical OECD-stated country expense of US$11,512 (OECD 2008, 219).

Financial aid: the United States is perceived as a prosperous and generous country, with 25.9 percent of international students indicating their U.S. university as their primary source of funding (IIE 2008).

Recent Changes

More institutions actively recruiting: the Council of International Schools (CIS) and Linden Educational Tours confirm that more U.S. colleges and universities traveled overseas with their organizations to recruit international students in 2008 than they did 10 years ago. They also noted a greater variety of participating universities—Big Ten and Ivy League universities, community colleges, art and design schools, law schools, and business schools.

Changing regulations: specifically, the United States has issued an interim final rule increasing the Optional Practical Training (OPT) program to 29 months for graduates of STEM (science, technology, engineering, and mathematics) disciplines, thereby encouraging students in these areas to study (and work) in the United States.

Recognizing three-year degrees for graduate study: the Council of Graduate Schools (CGS 2006) reported in its *2006 CGS International Graduate Admissions Survey* that 56 percent of polled schools said the three-year European bachelor's degrees were not problematic; that nearly 50 percent had adopted policies evaluating the three-year degree as equivalent to a U.S. bachelor's degree; and another nearly 30 percent stated that they did not reject the three-year degrees but evaluated each applicant on an individual basis regardless of degree length.

Graduate deans get involved: the Council of Graduate Schools reported that in 2008, 81 percent of graduate deans undertook one or more recruitment efforts; 54 percent worked with foreign institutions or consortia to identify potential students; and 31 percent devoted more funding for overseas recruitment trips (CGS 2008).

Stronger alumni programs: universities are building and strengthening their international student alumni programs, and alumni are more engaged in encouraging students to apply to their alma mater.

Faculty exchanges: the American Council on Education reports significant increases in the percentages of faculty leading education abroad programs, attending meetings overseas, and conducting research in other countries and notes that "faculty play a leading role in driving campus internationalization."(Koch 2008).

Government funding: through the U.S. State Department EducationUSA centers and the Department of Commerce International Trade Administration, the U.S. government has put additional resources into promoting U.S. universities abroad.

Presidential election: the election of Barack Obama has sent a signal that the United States is a welcoming, dynamic, pluralistic society that intends to invest in young people.

Future Considerations

The 2008-09 global financial situation may see the demise of some of the newer institutions and joint venture programs, while at the same time creating truly fierce competition among the major receiving countries, i.e., the United States, the United Kingdom, Australia, and Canada.

As a growing percentage of students come from India, China, and Korea, U.S. universities will have to confront the issue of diversity (or lack thereof) in their international student population.

Vitality, quality, diversity, and financial aid remain the keys to attracting international students so these factors must be protected, maintained, and improved in the face of economic distress and protectionist sentiment.

A realistic, transparent, and workable student visa system that encourages talented students to study in the United States before dealing with their career options would be the best silver bullet for attracting international students to U.S campuses. This is also true for the many other countries also implementing more stringent visa regulations.

In a world where national boundaries are fading in the social, financial, and business communities—and yet ethnic, religious, and political differences still persist—the United States, as with all countries, must reach out to students from around the world. Colleges and universities should invite them to their campuses, engage them in learning and teaching, and send them out to work for a more civil and civilized society. International students bring dollars, talent, culture, diversity, vitality, and different ways of looking at the world to the classroom and the community. They enrich the institution, broaden the horizons of their classmates, and are an essential part of maintaining the nation's global leadership. U.S. universities will continue to attract the brightest students from around the world if they uphold their standards and work cooperatively on campus, within their community, and with their government. It is a task well worth pursuing.

Bibliography

Banks, Melissa, Alan Olsen, and David Pearce. 2007. *Global Student Mobility: An Australian Perspective Five Years On.* Canberra: IDP Education

Center for World-Class Universities. 2008. *"2008 Academic Ranking of World Universities."* Shanghai Jiao Tong University. www.arwu.org/rank2008/EN2008.htm.

Council of Graduate Schools (CGS). 2006. *Findings from the 2006 CGS International Graduate Admissions Survey, Phase III: Admissions and Enrollment.* October 2006, revised March 2007. http://www.cgsnet.org/portals/0/pdf/R_Intlenrl06_III.pdf.

Council of Graduate Schools (CGS). 2008. *Findings from the 2008 CGS International Graduate Admissions Survey, Phase III: Final Offers of Admission and Enrollment.* November 2008. www.cgsnet.org/portals/0/pdf/R_IntlEnrl08_III.pdf.

Institute of International Education (IIE). 2008. *Open Doors 2008: Report on International Educational Exchange.* New York: Institute of International Education.

Institute of International Education (IIE). 2008. "Global Destinations for International Students, Atlas of Social Mobility." *Project Atlas.* www.atlas.iienetwork.org/?p = 48027

Koch, Kimberly. 2008. "Internationalization in the U.S.: Slipping Backward?" *International Higher Education* Number 53, Fall 2008.

Organisation for Economic Co-operation and Development (OECD). 2008. *Education at a Glance 2008: OECD Indicators.* www.oecd.org/dataoecd/23/46/41284038.pdf.

Sirkin, Hal, Jim Hemerling, and Arindam Bhattacharya. 2008. *Globality: Competing with Everyone from Everywhere for Everything.* New York: Business Plus, Hatchett Book Group

Wooldridge, Adrian. 2006. "The Battle for Brain Power." *The Economist* October 5.

West, Charlotte. 2008. "Building International Brands." *International Educator* 17, 5.

Background

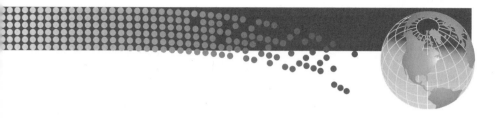

A Brief History of International Recruitment in U.S. Higher Education

Stephen C. Dunnett

At most U.S. colleges and universities, international recruitment has become a formal, stand-alone administrative endeavor only within the past two decades, as competition for international students and the perceived benefits they offer to postsecondary institutions has markedly increased. Previously, relatively few institutions had any programs aimed at recruiting students from other countries. Those that did typically were private colleges that recruited international students to diversify their enrollment.

The Early Years (1960s–1970s)

In the 1960s and 1970s the number of self-funded international students grew dramatically worldwide, thanks largely to improvements in the economies and education systems of many developing countries. Despite steep increases in real tuition charges at U.S. colleges and universities and decreases in financial aid from the federal government, international student enrollments increased rapidly—from 53,107 in 1960 to 336,985 in 1982.

Although the pool of eligible students abroad expanded rapidly, demographic changes in the United States reduced domestic enrollments at many institutions. By the mid-1970s senior administrators and admission officers were responding to anticipated declines in enrollments of traditional college-age students and seeking ways to compensate for the shortfall.

The decline in the rate of growth of domestic enrollments occurred during an era of increasing fiscal austerity for many colleges and universities. Under growing pressure to maintain enrollments and boost tuition revenue, many institutions closed, retrenched, or refashioned themselves to serve new markets during this period. Aggressive recruitment programs were undertaken, and, as costs went up, financial aid awards also increased to ensure that students continued to enroll. Although enrollments increased somewhat in the late 1970s, the enrollment prospects for the future were not encouraging. In addition, the number of post-secondary institutions in the United States increased from 2,556 in 1970 to 3,231 in 1980 to more than 3,500 in 1990, making competition for students even more fierce. The one bright spot in the forecast was the projection that international student enrollments would continue to increase rapidly throughout the 1980s, as indeed they did.

Seeing self-funded international students as one way to address enrollment problems, institutions began to look more seriously at overseas recruitment. Initially, the resulting recruitment activities did not serve the ultimate mission of the institutions nor were they in the best interests of the international students who were recruited.

Setting Recruitment Standards

The mid-1970s to the mid-1980s marked not only the beginning of large-scale overseas recruitment efforts by many institutions, but also the proliferation of third party recruiters who often charged a fee to help international students gain admission to an American college or university.

During that decade, as the profitable business of third party recruiting expanded, so did the possibilities for abuse. Unethical recruitment practices, incidences of gross misrepresentation of American higher education overseas, and violations of U.S. immigration laws led to growing criticism by students, parents, and officials overseas as well as by educators and the general public in the United States.

Several high-level efforts to investigate recruitment practices and propose ethical standards for international recruitment were organized. The most important of these was the Wingspread Colloquium, held in March of 1980, which addressed the topic Foreign Student Recruitment: Realities and Recommendations. Sponsored by the National Liaison Committee on Foreign Student Admissions—a coalition made up of NAFSA, the American Association of Collegiate Registrars and Admissions Officers (AACRAO), the Institute of International Education (IIE), the Council of Graduate Schools, and the College Board—the colloquium was attended by international students, admission officers, overseas educational advisers, international student advisers, and representatives of professional organizations, consortia, and government agencies.

Although the colloquium focused primarily on the problems associated with the recruitment and admission of international students, it did not recommend a reduction in the flow of students coming to the United States from abroad. Rather, it called for more responsible and effective oversight of the process of directing students to suitable U.S. institutions, a curb on the abuses, and the promotion of professional and institutional standards for ethical recruitment. A set of criteria was put forward as a basis for promoting ethical recruitment practices. These criteria stipulated that institutions of higher education were required to provide prospective international students with accurate and adequate information about their institutions; their programs, costs, and support service; and about U.S. higher education in general—to enable students to make well-informed decisions when seeking admission.

In addition, the criteria called for the establishment of effective institutional policies on international student recruitment, admission, and support services, and also advocated restricting the evaluation of foreign academic credentials to suitably qualified admission professionals. In addressing the controversial practice of paying agents for each student recruited, the colloquium recommended that institutions "avoid contractual arrangements with agents who require fee-for-enrollment payments."

The recommendations of the Wingspread Colloquium formed the basis for NAFSA's first statement and guidelines for ethical recruitment. The early recommendations were subsequently revised and updated according to the needs of both international students and U.S. higher education. The current NAFSA Statement of Ethical Principles is available at www.nafsa.org/ethics.

Recruitment Activities: Tours and Fairs

Some forward-looking U.S. colleges and universities began formal recruitment and international student scholarship programs in the 1970s. In the late 1970s and early 1980s, IIE sponsored educational tours to multiple Asian countries for university administrators. The purpose of the IIE program was to help U.S. administrators learn more about Asian educational systems and at the same time provide an opportunity for Asian students to get some first-hand information from U.S. college and university administrators. Those tours laid the foundation for future group travel and recruitment in Asia.

When international enrollments first began to level off in the mid-1980s and competition for international students grew more intense, more admission offices began employing recruitment techniques that had been developed to recruit domestic students. Admission staff created promotional publications and other admission materials specifically for international students, participated in the growing number of university fairs, established extensive contacts with a network of local schools and overseas educational advisers, enlisted the help of faculty and alumni in foreign countries to meet with prospective students, and developed sophisticated databases and tracking systems to ensure better oversight of the admission process from initial contact to enrollment.

Overseas recruitment tours for admission representatives became an essential component of international recruitment programs. In 1972 the European Council of International Schools (ECIS) conducted the first recruitment tour of Europe for U.S. colleges and universities. The purpose of the tour, which involved some fifteen U.S. institutions, was to facilitate students in international schools in Europe meeting directly with U.S. admission representatives.

Similarly, in 1982 the College Information Exchange organized a tour to Latin America at the request of guidance counselors in Central and South America who wanted their students to have direct access to U.S. admission officers. That was also the year in which Linden Educational Services first conducted a recruitment tour of Asia, and IIE discontinued its educational tours for university administrators.

The Growth Years (1980s–1990s)

During the 1980s, the goal of internationalizing U.S. higher education by "importing" international students was part of a larger vision articulated by some educators who called on colleges and universities to overcome their provincialism and adopt a global perspective. Their aims were to better prepare their students, to foster mutually beneficial exchanges and collaborative activities with partner institutions abroad, and ultimately to promote better cooperation and understanding between the United States and other countries.

Although they were less vulnerable to the demographic changes affecting undergraduate enrollment, research universities faced their own challenges. It became increasingly difficult in the 1980s to recruit enough qualified students into science and engineering graduate programs. To maintain these programs and to continue their extensive research endeavors, academic departments, especially in the Sciences, Technology, Engineering, and Math (STEM) disciplines, looked to international students to make up for the enrollment shortfall. Over time, international students came to dominate many graduate programs in these fields, in some cases representing 70 percent or more of the enrollment. Without them, many of these programs could not have been sustained. Regrettably this situation continues today.

At the same time, administrators of large and/or prestigious universities took it for granted that ever-increasing numbers of international students would come to the United States without special recruitment efforts because of the appeal of U.S. higher education: superior programs, faculty, and facilities; as well as openness, accessibility, and flexibility. They believed international students did not have choices. This complacency would later be challenged as students in key markets such as Asia began to be recruited in larger numbers by institutions in other countries, notably Britain and Australia.

As the number of self-funded international students coming to the United States grew, the costs of higher education became an increasingly important factor in their enrollment decisions and hence in recruitment strategies. Although it is not clear how many prospective international students were prevented from enrolling because of high costs, the proportion of those enrolling in public universities, where tuition is lower, clearly increased over time. Soon higher education was a leading American export, representing billions of dollars in revenue not only to colleges and universities, but also to the localities in which international students resided.

The 1990s witnessed a growing number of U.S. colleges and universities engaged in international student recruitment. New technology, entrepreneurial organizations, enrollment management techniques, fiscal constraints at institutions, and increasing competition from other countries combined to produce a robust yet challenging landscape for U.S. institutions interested in enrolling international students.

During this decade, international recruitment became big business, with a variety of consultants, professional organizations, and for-profit companies providing a wide range of services, both in the United States and abroad, to colleges and universities. These services included professional development workshops; marketing and enrollment-management consultancy; organized recruitment tours to different countries and regions; advising and referral services; credential evaluation services; advertising and publicity in print, video, and electronic media; and hardware and software development to facilitate admission and enrollment management functions. As they developed more organized and systematic international recruitment programs, colleges and universities were better able to track and manage their international enrollments to meet their institutional objectives.

In keeping with more innovative management practices, many campuses set up centralized offices of "enrollment management," headed by senior administrators often at the vice president or vice provost level. Originating as an extension of the admissions office, enrollment management came to encompass many other areas, including retention, financial aid, student service, and academic advisement (Dixon 1995). These enrollment management offices were mainly charged with the recruitment of domestic students; however, the more progressive offices came to view international recruitment as an integral part of a comprehensive enrollment management plan.

During this period international recruitment was increasingly facilitated by the development of information technologies that made possible not only instant communication by e-mail, fax, and the Internet with students in remote locations, but also by greater efficiencies in the admission process. In particular, the Internet has become an invaluable recruitment tool, allowing ready access for many students overseas to a broad range of up-to-date campus information and contacts, as well as online application. In the twenty-year period from 1982 through 2001, international enrollments in the U.S. greatly expanded, from 336,985 to 582,996—an increase of nearly 75 percent.

The 1990s were also an era of financial austerity and cutbacks, especially for public institutions, which in some cases looked toward higher tuition charged to international students as a vital revenue stream. At the same time the number of 18-year-olds began to decline in the U.S., the number of international students in U.S. postsecondary education leveled off, around 450,000 in the mid-1990s, and competition for students heated up, recruitment activities became even more aggressive, and enrollment managers scrambled to keep up with the changing circumstances.

The financial crisis that struck East and Southeast Asia in the mid- to late-1990s came as a rude awakening to institutions that had become dependent on enrollments of students from Asia. For much of the previous two decades, between 50 and 60 percent of all international students in U.S. postsecondary education had come from Asia. In 1996-97, according to *Open Doors,* the annual census of international student flows to and from the United States, Canada was the only non-Asian country on the list of the top ten countries of origin. Many intensive English programs were particularly reliant on Asian students and, therefore, more vulnerable to the crisis.

The situation in Asia demonstrated once again the fluidity of the international student market and reminded institutions to diversify their overseas recruitment efforts to include other promising markets such as Latin America, Central and Eastern Europe, Russia, Eurasia, Turkey, and India. Even before the financial difficulties in Asia, educators at many U.S. colleges and universities saw the need to diversify their enrollments to achieve a better mix of students on campus, to afford their international students and all students a more satisfying educational experience, and to ensure better retention and graduation rates.

At the same time, the international student market began to change, and those changes continue today. Most notable of those is the sharp increase in the number of students studying outside their home countries. The British Council (2003) has projected that the demand for international higher education will increase from 2.1 million places in 2003 to approximately 6 million by 2020. Other studies project even greater numbers during the next 10–15 years. However, competition for international students has also increased as the United Kingdom, Canada, France, Germany, and especially Australia have aggressively recruited international students to their institutions of higher education. Many of these countries stepped up their international recruitment activities after September 11, resulting in overseas students beginning to realize they had choices. Thanks to the information provided by these recruiters, overseas students began to realize other countries had higher education facilities and academic programs equal or superior to those of the U.S., and at a significantly lower cost.

The Post-September 11 Period

The terrorist attacks of September 11, 2001 forever changed international education in the United States. In the aftermath of September 11, the U.S. government imposed a number of security measures that resulted in stricter international student visa controls and lengthy background security checks on international student and scholar applicants. These measures and other factors resulted in a subsequent decline in the number of international students beginning their education in the United States. Although the Department of State has worked hard to streamline visa issuance procedures and to assure overseas students that the United States is open and welcoming, growth has been anemic, especially when compared with other countries. Between 1999 and 2005, international enrollment in the U.S. grew by 17 percent, whereas international enrollment grew by 29 percent in the United Kingdom, 42 percent in Australia, 46 percent in Germany, and 81 percent in France during the same period.

Other factors also played a role in the decline in number of international students coming to the United States during the early 2000s. One factor is the increased access to higher education, especially in Asia, where newly affluent countries expanded and improved their systems of higher education. Many Asian students now have access to world-class higher education at home. Another factor is the proliferation of degree programs taught in English in France, Germany, and China, as well as other countries. However, the greatest factor affecting U.S. enrollments is the entrance of new players into the international education market; in particular, Singapore, Malaysia, and even China have begun to promote themselves as regional and highly affordable hubs for world-class higher education. The result is that there are now, for example, more Japanese and Korean students studying in China than in the United States.

Since the early 2000s, many overseas institutions have begun to differentiate themselves, not only from one another, but also from their U.S. counterparts, in an aggressive effort to attract a larger share of the growing overseas student market. Their admission processes are less complicated and time consuming than those of the United States, and obtaining student visas is much less burdensome and expensive. Some countries, such as Canada and Singapore, for example, allow international students to work part time off campus, and even encourage international students to apply for permanent residence upon completion of their studies. The possibility of working in the host country is a major motivation for many international students in their choice of country for education. For some time the U.S. has allowed graduating students the possibility of engaging in a one-year practical training work experience. In 2008 international students enrolled in STEM fields in U.S. universities will be allowed to extend their one-year practical training to 17 months. This will certainly make the U.S. more attractive to overseas students.

After a period of initial confusion immediately following September 11, many U.S. universities and colleges sharply stepped up their international student recruitment efforts. Many of them established stand-alone international enrollment management offices dedicated to increasing the enrollment of international students through recruitment activities in other countries, to managing the admission and enrollment process of international students, and to working with academic units on the campus to meet international student enrollment targets, while ensuring the retention of recruited students. Staff in these international enrollment management offices quickly developed long-term institutional international enrollment plans. They streamlined and improved their existing admission procedures and reduced their processing times. They began to send staff on carefully targeted overseas recruitment trips where they participated in an ever-growing number and variety of fairs and seminars. They also worked hard to improve services for international students on the home campus to improve retention. Another important function of offices of international enrollment management has been to make the on-campus case for the importance of international students to the institution.

U.S. institutions of higher education have also started to develop collaborative academic agreements with overseas institutions such as undergraduate 2 + 2 transfer programs whereby students spend two years in their home country and then complete their degree in two years in the United States, dual degrees, and overseas branch campuses, all in an effort to ensure a steady stream of international students to the home campus. These relationships have also been helpful in providing education abroad opportunities for domestic students.

International student recruitment today has now become not only a big business, but a highly professional one on many U.S. college and university campuses. It has also been very successful, indicated by international enrollments at many institutions having stabilized and even increased. U.S. colleges and universities have learned that they cannot be complacent and expect international students to apply on their own. Most U.S. colleges and universities must compete actively for each and every international student, and competition will only intensify in the future as the number of countries and institutions worldwide become involved in international recruitment. If U.S. higher education is to maintain its preeminence as a destination for international students, then U.S. colleges and universities will need to be more strategic and proactive in recruiting students from overseas.

Bibliography

Baer, Michael A., and Peter A. Stace. 1997. "Enrollment Management." In *First Among Equals: The Role of the Chief Academic Officer,* ed. James Martin et al. Baltimore: Johns Hopkins University Press.

British Council. 2003. *Vision 2020: Forecasting International Student Mobility – A UK Perspective.*

Dixon, Rebecca R. 1995. "What Is Enrollment Management?" In *Making Enrollment Management Work,* ed. Rebecca R. Dixon. San Francisco: Jossey-Bass.

Goodwin, Craufurd D., and Michael Nacht. 1983. *Absence of Decision: Foreign Students in American Colleges and Universities.* New York: Institute of International Education.

NAFSA Statement of Ethical Principles. 2009. www.nafsa.org/ethics.

Open Doors: Report on International Educational Exchange. 1996-97. New York: Institute of International Education.

Verbik, Line, and Veronica Lasanowski. 2007. *International Student Mobility: Patterns and Trends.* London: The Observatory on Borderless Higher Education.

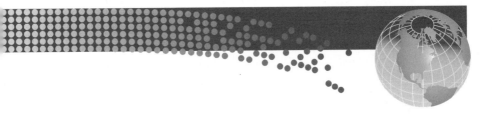

Ethics in International Student Recruitment

Linda Heaney and Panetha Theodosia Nychis Ott

Like domestic admission, international student recruitment is grounded in a set of well-understood principles. It begins with a commitment from the institution, often noted in its mission statement, to value international students and their contributions to the student body and to provide them with the programs and services they need to succeed.

The recruitment process requires constant vigilance because abuses have taken place and continue to happen, albeit in very small numbers. The root cause is ignorance or naiveté—of foreign students who are vulnerable to misinformation, of administrators looking for easy answers to difficult enrollment questions, of admission representatives insufficiently trained in evaluating international credentials, and of representatives of the institution not familiar with the NAFSA Statement of Ethical Principles (www.nafsa.org/ethics).

This chapter describes NAFSA's role in ethical issues, highlights the key ethical challenges in international student recruitment, and concludes with a list of best practices for institutions and individual admissions officers.

NAFSA's Role in Ethical Recruitment

NAFSA, during the past few decades, has examined and reexamined the role of ethics in international recruitment and has codified a set of principles so that its members can always keep in mind the necessity of appropriate rules of conduct in all interactions. As an organization NAFSA has collected and studied cases in which the solution to issues was not always clear or where there was a perceived conflict of interest. In its most recent version, approved by the Board of Directors in March 2009, NAFSA produced a statement that includes best practices in the form of a code of honor to which all international recruiters should adhere in their work with students and scholars. The principles are fundamental best practices. Expectations include integrity and fairness, respect for laws and regulations, quality in services provided, competence and professionalism, respect for and understanding of the diversity of thought and perspectives of people from different cultures, transparency in dealings with others, access, and responsiveness. At its root, the Statement of Ethical Principles is a reminder that the needs and the welfare of international students and scholars should govern the actions of international recruiters and should be the primary consideration.

Very often we may feel that we are faced with conflicts of interest between institutional needs and the welfare of international students. The Statement of Ethical Principles serves to provide a guideline for international recruiters when faced with such conflicts.

Challenges in the Recruitment of International Students

Due to pressure on institutions to increase enrollments and generate revenues, coupled with demands from alumni/ae, donors, and board members to foster a more global outlook on campus, there are several key challenges that need constant attention.

Complete and Accurate Information

International students need not only complete, accurate, and current information but also a context in which to place that information. Institutions should be clear about what they are offering international applicants. Consider, for example, an international student admitted to a pre-engineering program. The student should be informed that transfer to an engineering school may be required after two or three years of pre-engineering study, that transfer may not be automatic, and that procedures will have to be followed to complete the transfer. If credit is given for previous studies, students should be informed about how many of these credits count toward the degree, and whether the student will have to meet a residency requirement to obtain the degree.

Putting the Information into Context

Providing a context for information is particularly important in matters relating to costs and financial assistance. Students who hear about the minimum wage in the United States sometimes think they can live on this amount if they can get 20 hours of work a week. They also think it's possible to live miles from the campus and rely on public transportation. Because many international students cannot realistically grasp the costs related to health care, they do not understand the necessity of having health insurance. Students need a context in which to put the numbers.

Scholarships and Financial Aid

It is the university's responsibility to provide complete and accurate information about financial support opportunities so that students can make an informed choice. When prospective applicants indicate that they need full financial assistance but receive application forms and literature that omit this important policy information, students frequently assume financial aid is available. Unfortunately, they then spend time and money applying to a school they cannot afford to attend.

Third-Party Representation of Students

In many countries, it is customary to use a go-between to accomplish difficult tasks. Therefore, it is a best practice to have the student sign the application, know all of the costs of attending the institution and independently verify all transcripts with the institution that issued the document.

Institutions and agents are expected to remember that the best interest of the student should govern their practices in recruitment and matriculation. (See also Chapter 4.4, Working with Third-Party Agents, and the NAFSA practice resource, Working with Agents, www.nafsa.org/knowledge_community_network. sec/recruitment_admissions/recruiting_and_marketing/practice_resources_2/ working_with_agents_2.)

On-the-Spot Admission

Because British and Australian universities have stepped up their recruitment efforts and offer "on-the-spot" admission, more students are demanding immediate rulings on admission decisions. U.S. government regulations require admission decisions be made at the institution's U.S. location, and that the university obtain a written application, the student's transcript, and other records of courses taken, proof of adequate financial resources, and other supporting documents before making the decision.

Proactive and Professional Ethical Recruitment Practices

An Effective International Admissions Office

- Has a strong commitment to student service and development;

- Has a clear understanding of institutional mission, policies and standards;

- Communicates clearly with prospective international students about the institution, admission requirements and admission procedures, and uses communication media effectively to promote and manage the admissions process;

- Recruits and/or conducts outreach activities ethically and with the aim of attracting candidates for admission whose profile is consistent with the offerings and goals of the institution;

- Responsibly manages record keeping according to accepted professional standards, and considers differences in document-issuing practices around the world;

- Evaluates foreign educational documentation accurately and fairly, in a manner consistent with the institution's academic profile and mission, and based on research and application of standard evaluation methodology and principles; or responsibly outsources foreign credential evaluation;

- Coordinates and cooperates with other offices or functions of the institution that are involved in the admissions process;

- Understands the relationship between the admissions process and require- ments of the immigration-regulating branches of the U.S. government, as appropriate to the student population it serves, and performs required func- tions lawfully and accurately, in a timely manner and with the best interest of both the student and the institution in mind;

- Trains its staff and supports continuing education and professional develop- ment of staff members;

- Provides the financial, material, and human resources needed to perform its duties effectively and efficiently;

- Assesses the effectiveness of admission policy and processing on a regular basis and makes adjustments as necessary, in the context of institutional mission and goals; and

- Is committed to the goals of international education and exchange.

A Professional Admissions Officer

- Knows that ethical behavior and standards are a part of the job;

- Recognizes that if ethical standards are maintained, both the student and the institution will benefit;

- Educates colleagues and senior administration about the need for main- taining ethical standards. One of the best ways to do this is to keep the administration aware of changes in the international student market so they can be prepared for changing enrollments;

- Remembers that ethical standards are tested when enrollment targets are not being met;

- Monitors closely the work of alumni and others who represent the institution;

- Reviews written materials to see that they portray the institution accurately;

- Thinks about how much time must be devoted to borderline or failing students and makes every effort to admit only those students who meet the stated admission criteria;

- Understands the difference between a placement agency that works on behalf of the student and an agency that recruits for the institution. Individuals who do both will, sooner or later, make a less-than-perfect match;

- Requires agencies to become thoroughly familiar with the institution and its students, and limits the scope of what the agent can and cannot do for the institution.

- Remembers that appearances matter; and

- Holds meetings at least annually between decisionmakers and those who actively recruit overseas to assess results, discuss lessons learned, and make future plans.

The winning combination is a student who thoughtfully chooses to enroll in an institution, knowing that he is well qualified and excited about the course offerings and campus environment, and an institution that proudly graduates a student from another country. This can only happen when admissions offices maintain the highest of standards and international student recruiters do their job in a professional manner.

Resources

NAFSA Adviser's Manual Online. NAFSA: Association of International Educators. Annual subscription to content of online publication. www.nafsa.org/themanual.

NAFSA Statement of Ethical Principles. 2009. www.nafsa.org/ethics.

Getting Ready to Recruit

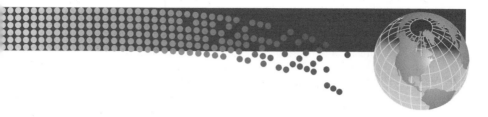

Preparing to Recruit

Negar Davis

Recruiting international students is not as simple as one may think. A successful recruitment initiative hinges upon thinking ahead and preparing the campus and the community for enrolling and hosting international students. The institution that approaches recruiting with a clear strategic vision with articulated goals and outcomes, and with the commitment to provide the necessary infrastructure for the increased number of students on campus, will stand a much better chance of success than the organization that approaches this task naively, haphazardly, ad hoc, or without campus and community-wide buy in.

Campus and Community Services

The following inventory of campus and community services serve as a preliminary checklist for institutions considering international student recruitment. International students will impact many other campus services, but these, at minimum, must be in place.

Admission

An institution's admission office plays a critical role in enrollment management including policy decisions (e.g., setting standards for admission); planning and participating in recruitment activities; developing, printing, and mailing materials; advising prospective students; processing and evaluating applications for admission; and conducting research relating to the recruitment and admission of students.

- Will additional staff be needed to respond to application requests from abroad? Will it be necessary to employ such staff year round, or will the demands be seasonal?

- What is an acceptable turnaround time for applications? Will additional staff be needed to process and evaluate applications in a timely manner?

- Will the admission office have the capacity to handle requests from academic departments for more detailed information on students' educational backgrounds for purposes of admission and advising?

- Has your school developed an application form targeted at specifically suited for international students? If so, is the form adequate? Your office may face a deluge of inquiries if the form does not address the needs and concerns of its international audience.

- Are your publications competitive? Internet and print are avenues for reaching potential students. Does your institution have a recruiting DVD designed for international students? Does your institution's Web home page have an international presence?

- Should you consider developing country-specific applications and recruiting materials?

- Should you consider utilizing Facebook, blogs, text messaging, and other forms of communication to prospective students? If so, do you have staff to perform these tasks, and update and monitor information?

- Will the admission office need to expand its library of materials on the educational systems of other countries? These references might include books, newsletters, periodicals, electronic resources, and information gained from professional conferences. Is there a budget for such things?

Grants and Scholarships

Schools interested in recruiting international students may consider offering financial incentives to attract high-quality applicants. In addition to grants from institutional resources, other forms of student assistance can be explored such as scholarships based on financial need and through endowments and other awards. International students are not eligible for federal financial aid, and employment opportunities are limited by immigration regulations.

- Should financial aid be used as a tool to recruit international students? If so, who will supply the funding? Will the scholarships be awarded on the basis of merit or need? Especially with regard to the latter, what criteria would be used to judge applicants?

- Is there an adequate supply of on-campus jobs from which international students might earn some spending money and contribute to payment of their expenses? Are graduate assistantships available, and do they pay a high enough salary to support a single student's education?

- Is there an emergency loan fund or source of emergency grants for students who experience unanticipated financial difficulty? If not, can such a fund be created and can it grow to accommodate an inevitable increase in applicants?

English as a Second Language

Many colleges and universities offer several levels of English as a Second Language (ESL) programs, from conventional "intensive" study programs for nondegree-seeking students to remedial coursework for degree-seeking students, and special programs to certify graduate teaching assistants' English-language proficiency levels.

- Can a method be developed to predict accurately the number of new students who will need to be tested for placement in these programs?

- Will there be provision for adequate space and staff for testing new students?

- Will there be funds to increase the number of ESL sections offered in proportion to any increase in enrollment? Will there be adequate faculty, course offerings, and course levels?

- Will additional clerical support be available for an expanded ESL program?

- Will there be physical space to build and grow the program?

- Should intensive English students be allowed to take some academic coursework before completing their course of English study? How will the level of proficiency that will qualify them for concurrent academic coursework be determined?

- If you have no plans to offer ESL assistance, is such assistance readily available in your community, perhaps at another institution with which you may be able to form a partnership?

- Will an adequate number of remedial ESL courses be offered for those students whose academic performance would be compromised without additional ESL work?

- Will academic support and remedial services include assistance in writing, conversational English, and reading?

International Student Services

The international student services (ISS) office handles activities related to the regulatory and well-being needs of international students on campus. The philosophical stance an office takes toward its clients can have a huge impact on the success or failure of recruiting and enrollment efforts. Some offices view themselves as deputized branches of the Department of Homeland Security (DHS) and concentrate on tracking students in an effort to monitor their activities. Other offices concentrate their resources on enhancing the academic, social, and personal experiences of international students on campus and making their stay as comfortable and productive as possible. Ideally these offices should handle both to provide a home away from home atmosphere.

Staffing needs in the ISS office will depend not only on the philosophical stance that office takes toward its clients, but also on the clients themselves. The volume and nature of the ISS office's work will vary with the size and composition of the international student population and in response to unpredictable global events.

Will staffing be adequate to meet the anticipated demands of an increased international student population?

- What role will the ISS office play in the development of needed services for an influx of students? Will the office attempt to provide such services, or will the office attempt to "mainstream" students by coordinating services with existing campus units?

- What types of programs will be offered by the ISS office? Will there be orientation for new students upon arrival? Will there be ongoing programming designed to facilitate cross-cultural learning? Will there be cocurricular programming that integrates international students into the campus community and recognizes them as a valuable learning resource?

- Will the international student advising staff initiate campus-wide training programs to sensitize U.S. staff to the needs and concerns of international students and thereby create a more understanding environment? Will such training address cross-cultural communication skills and dispute mediation?

- How will the ISS office cope with the added workload of immigration advising that an increase in students will bring?

Health Care and Insurance

International students are frequently baffled by the U.S. health care system because they often come from countries whose governments subsidize health care and insurance. There may be resentment toward campus policies that mandate insurance coverage or health screenings. Furthermore, the clinical paradigm learned at U.S. medical schools may confuse or offend international students. U.S. medical personnel may perform different roles than medical personnel in an international student's home country.

- Will health insurance be mandatory for international students? If so, how will the requirement be conveyed and justified? How will it be enforced?

- How will campus or community health service staff become sensitized to cross-cultural health issues?

- Will your school require any mandatory screening of international students (e.g., for tuberculosis, for hepatitis-B)? If so, how will the requirement be justified to new students? Will the health center commit more resources to staffing to implement those requirements? How will this be funded?

- If your campus has a counseling service, is it prepared for a possible influx of new students experiencing adjustment difficulties? Are staff trained to recognize and treat depression and other psychological conditions that might be manifested by students from other cultures?

- Will students with dependents be required to purchase insurance for their dependents as well? If so, how will that requirement be enforced?

- If more international students enroll at your institution, what will be the impact on broader health services in the community? Will free, walk-in clinics see an increase in international patients (either students or their dependents)? Will emergency treatment centers become de facto ambulatory clinics for international students or their dependents?

Academic Advising and Course Placement

Academic advising and course placement services are critical to new international students since most them are unfamiliar with the U.S. academic system. Availability of these services will make a huge difference, not only in the students' academic success or failure, but also in their general cultural adjustment.

- Will advisers be on duty or available during the weeks or days before the beginning of classes to advise new international students?

- If academic advising is centralized at the undergraduate level or within graduate departments, will there be enough advising staff to accommodate an increased population of international students?

- Will such staff have some familiarity with foreign credentials so that proper course placement is assured?

- Will the academic advisers be comfortable talking with people from other countries, or will some cross-cultural communication training needed?

- Will advisers have the ability to track student progress and make mid-course corrections in curricular selections during the student's program?

- Will an increase in international students be mirrored by an increase in course availability, especially in those majors that attract large numbers of students?

Career Services and Placement

As competition for international students intensifies, it becomes increasingly important that students believe they are receiving a good return on their investment. For many, the most concrete result of their U.S. education may be employment after graduation.

- Does the placement office at your college serve the needs of international students? For example, is there timely information about opportunities abroad?

- Does the staff focus mailings or newsletters to international students?

- Are placement counselors informed about federal regulations affecting employment in the United States for students from abroad?

- Does the international student services office meet routinely with the placement office to exchange information and discuss concerns?

Housing

Housing issues can be divided into on-campus and off-campus concerns. The degree to which either is predominant will depend on the type of institution (e.g., commuter, small private college with residence hall residency requirements, large institution) and the size of the community in which it is located (small town with limited off-campus housing versus city with ample off-campus housing within commuting distance).

- What temporary housing, if any, will the institution offer to new international students as they seek off-campus housing or wait for on-campus housing contracts to begin?

- Should an international residence hall (or an international wing or floor) be established in an effort to recruit international students to the school and into the residence hall system?

- Should a segment of a residence hall be set aside for upper division or graduate students to make residence hall living more appealing to them?

- Will residence hall staff, particularly resident assistants who live on the floors, be given adequate training to deal with cross-cultural misunderstanding and conflict that may arise between American and international roommates?

- Will residence halls provide programming designed to increase understanding of cross-cultural issues?

- Will there be consideration with regard to religious and dietary needs?

- If there is family housing available on the campus, is there a community center for educational and social activities that would encourage interactions between international and U.S. families?

- Will students interested in living off-campus be provided assistance in looking for suitable housing?

- Does the school or the community sponsor a tenant-landlord association that can recommend standards of housing, legal wording in leases, and dispute resolution in cases of disagreement or misunderstanding?

Needs of Dependents

Many international students are professionals, government officials, and/or post-doctoral students seeking research experience in the United States; in other words, they may be older, married and have young families. Since dependents cannot work legally (the exception being dependents in J-2 status), and many arrive with limited English and full responsibility for child-care, the spouses of international students are often very vulnerable to isolation and culture shock.

- Will affordable, temporary housing be available while families search for appropriate permanent housing?

- Is inexpensive or free ESL instruction available for spouses who may need it to manage day-to-day functioning in the local community.

- Does your community have enough day care facilities to support a sudden influx of children from other countries? Is it affordable for students, who frequently live at or near the poverty line?

- Does the international office (or some other entity) sponsor an organization or activities for spouses of international student, ones that help them integrate into the campus and community and offer social support and practical assistance?

- Are community social services prepared for an influx of foreign dependents? For example, will private health care providers be in a position to respond adequately to patients with different cultural values, illnesses not normally encountered in your part of the world, and (perhaps) limited English proficiency? Are the various levels of health and human service associations briefed as to the eligibility requirements for access to their services (e.g., WIC, Medicaid, food stamps)? Is there a female physician practicing in the community?

- Can the local schools accommodate students from other countries? Does the school district offer ESL instruction?

A Winning Formula

The institution that plans ahead, thinks strategically, stays true to its mission, and involves campus and community players will serve international students and be rewarded with a robust global outlook where the winners are the students, faculty, and the community.

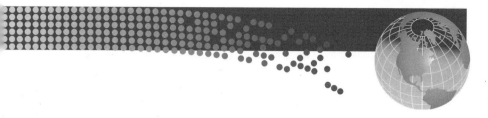

Creating a Strategic Plan

June Noronha

International student recruitment is more likely to succeed if it is done as a result of strategic planning rather than spontaneously or sporadically as a response to enrollment pressures. A strategic plan for international recruitment should be tied to the institution's overall plan for internationalization of the institution. Ideally, it should be a component of this plan, which would encompass education abroad, faculty engagement, international partnerships, staff-faculty exchanges, internationalizing the disciplines, and inter-institutional affiliations. At a minimum, it should be *linked* to the larger enrollment management plan of the institution.

Much has been published about strategic planning, including myriad models and frameworks. Traditional goals-based models coexist with more recent issues-based models. The goals-based model is the most common and starts with the organization's mission, goals that work toward mission strategies, and action planning to achieve the goals. The issues-based model examines issues facing the organization, with strategies and action plans to address the issues. Both increasingly focus on performance and outcomes, which are often used for enrollment management activities.

A good discussion of performance-based strategic planning as "a formal process designed to help an organization identify and maintain an optimal alignment with the most important elements of its environment" can be found in *Working Toward Strategic Change* (Dolence, Rowley, and Lujan 1997). Other lesser-used models are scenario-based planning, an alignment model used when organizations need to fine tune strategies, and an organic or self-organizing approach, focused on common values and "gradual learning by doing" rather than a more deductive process.

If a strategic planning model is already in use at your institution, adopt it because it is difficult to impose one system upon another. If there is no model, identify the method that will work best at your institution. This chapter addresses components of both goals-based and performance-based models. Most current strategic planning is based on goals; the other, however, seems well tuned to recruitment and enrollment planning. Your institution will have to determine an optimal strategy: staying with a time-tested model, blending models, or switching to one that best suits its type and vision.

Strategic Planning for International Admissions

An effective strategic plan provides a framework for strategic thinking, direction, and action leading to the achievement of consistent and planned results. For international recruitment, the strategic plan will clearly identify the program's unique niches and draw a map of how to successfully enroll appropriate students into the program. The plan will specify long-term goals and identify budget priorities.

The starting point for institutions with few or no international students is different than for those institutions with some or many. However, all need up-to-date strategic and operational plans that should embed flexibility, given that recruitment of international students occurs in a volatile and complex global market.

At institutions that are just beginning to recruit international students, it is important to develop all the elements of a strategic plan, and to have both a two- and a five-year strategy. The short-term strategy is required because of the volatility of the global environment and the need for flexibility in implementation. At institutions that have been recruiting international students for many years and want to increase international enrollment, current efforts should be evaluated and attention paid to those elements that have not been addressed adequately.

Strategic planning in higher education presents particular challenges because of the nature of its participatory governance and longer planning timelines. So in addition to the elements listed earlier, cornerstones of good planning must also include presidential leadership, shared governance, and a participatory process (Wilkinson, Taylor, Peterson and Machado-Taylor 2007).

Political Realities

The finest strategic plan will fail if attention is not paid to your institution's political environment. It is crucial to have the support of upper-level administrators who are usually in the best position to make decisions that will contribute to a positive outcome. The plan will be more successful if the wider campus community is engaged at an early stage so that all parties involved agree on the basic premises for recruiting and recognize the potential impact such efforts will have on the academic and social environments. This will ensure that the goals and objectives support, and perhaps even influence, larger strategic plans of the institution, and that budgetary support will be forthcoming when needed. Regardless of where the impetus to recruit international students comes from, responsibility for recruitment should fall with the enrollment management, admission, or international office.

Key Elements in Strategic Planning

The following are crucial elements of strategic planning:

- Environmental Scan

- Analysis and assessment of the external and internal environments

- Analysis of strengths, weaknesses, opportunities, and threats

- Development of mission and goals

- Identification of key performance indicators or measures of essential outcome

- Identification of objectives, an action plan, and accountability

- Identification of resources, needs, and expenditures (Dolence, Rowley, and Lujan 1997; Uhl 1983).

Environmental Scan

It is crucial to have solid data and information bases. Planning depends on the availability of appropriate information and an astute analysis of the key factors that influence student choices. Environmental scanning involves examining many different environments; a common acronym is STEEP—scanning of sociological/cultural, technological, economic, environment, and political environments. (Morrison, 1992). For international recruitment, scanning has to span the campus, community, state, country, and indeed, the world

Analysis and Assessment of the Internal and External Environment

The internal environment must be surveyed for strengths and weaknesses; the external environment for opportunities and threats. An internal strength might be an increase in applications; a weakness, high dependence on state support. Externally, new international partnerships may be an opportunity; growing competition among state schools a threat (Rowley, Lujan, and Dolence 1997).

Internal Assessment

Institutions must determine how and why students decide to study in the United States and what will lead them to choose your school or program. Begin with an internal assessment of the international students who have already chosen your program or a program similar to yours located in the same region.

- Gather information about your current international students and the international experience of your faculty.

- Gather information about your programs of study, departments, and colleges, and the relevance to international students' interests

- Develop and distribute a student questionnaire to assess the admission process, sources of information about your programs, and how and why various choices were made.

- Analyze demographic factors, including the level and fields of study, gender, financial support, country and region of origin, ESL needs, and so on.

- Compare this to data on international students studying in the United States and in your particular region of the country (*Open Doors* is a good source).

- Compare with similar data on your competitors.

- Examine and analyze the ethnic makeup of your campus and community.

External Assessment

To assess the external environment you must take into account global mobility trends. Consider social, economic, cultural, and political patterns, and evaluate how your program fits into those patterns. Will your program be attractive to urban students in emerging economies who face a lack of local higher education opportunities? To the increasing number of multinational families in capital cities around the world who prefer a U.S. education? To those who need short-term training in the allied health fields?

Become current with political and economic events worldwide, and study educational changes in other countries. Good sources of information include:

- International faculty

- Scholars and students

- Immigrant and international media

- Credential evaluation services newsletters

- Embassies and international associations

- Web sites and print media that focus on country-specific and world-wide economic trends (OECD, World Bank, RAND, *The Economist, Far Eastern Economic Review)*

- Web sites and print media that focus on educational trends (UNESCO-Education, OECD, *The Chronicle of Higher Education, Journal of Studies in International Education,* government and university-based research)

- State international trade offices

- Electronic databases (ABI Inform Global, ERIC, PAIS International)

Understand the value and attraction of U.S. higher education compared with that of other countries that educate international students (e.g., Australia, Canada, China, France, India, Japan, United Kingdom). Also compare U.S. higher education with the educational systems in the students' countries of origin.

- Recognize and evaluate historical links. For example, consider the attraction of British education for members of Commonwealth countries, or religious affiliations linking Catholic institutions.

- Realistically assess the value and attraction of your program within this global and international context. Do your master of business administration (M.B.A.) tuition rates compare favorably with those of Australia, for example?

- Realistically examine your competition within the United States. This is important because, given the large number of academic institutions and programs in this country, many institutions position themselves primarily locally or regionally. It is not unusual to find institutions competing regionally for domestic students, and nationally (or internationally) for international students.

- Realistically examine the impact of increasing numbers of off-shore campuses in strong economies (Middle East, Singapore)

- Be clear headed when learning from and assessing your competition, their offerings, their pricing, their success, and their share of international student enrollments.

A complete and effective assessment should yield a plan that clearly articulates your institution's strengths and weaknesses. The plan also will identify the most promising regions of the world and segments of international students who might consider applying to your institution. You will then have information to more realistically develop a mission and goals.

Analysis of Strengths, Weaknesses, Opportunities, and Threats

A very useful and simple framework to analyze an organization's Strengths and Weaknesses (internal environment), and the Opportunities and Threats (external environment) is a SWOT analysis. This analysis provides information that is helpful in matching the institution's resources and capabilities to the competitive environment in which it operates. It helps focus on capabilities that could provide a competitive advantage and new opportunities for growth or success.

This is a first step, because there are two sides to a SWOT analysis—one external and one internal—and the best strategy is to create alignment between the two. You do this by adding a TOWS analysis, which is an outside-in strategic (market-driven) framework, to the SWOT, which is an inside-out strategy (resource-driven) framework (www.mindtools.com).

Use the matrix below to match external opportunities and threats with your organizational internal strengths and weaknesses.

SWOT/TOWS Matrix		
	External/Outside Opportunities **(O)** 1. 2. 3. 4.	External/Outside Threats **(T)** 1. 2. 3. 4.
Internal/Resource Strengths **(S)** 1. 2. 3. 4.	**SO** *GOOD FIT* Strategies using **strengths** to *maximize* **opportunities.**	**ST** *REDUCE VULNERABILITY* Strategies using **strengths** to *minimize* **threats.**
Internal/Resource Weaknesses **(W)** 1. 2. 3. 4.	**WO** *OVERCOME WEAKNESS* Strategies *minimizing* **weaknesses** by taking advantage of **opportunities.**	**WT** *PROTECTIVE APPROACH* Strategies *minimizing* **weaknesses** and avoiding **threats.**

Development of Mission and Goals

It is useful to define your mission, both to establish clarity of purpose and to provide a point of reference for recruitment decisions. A mission statement might include statements about revenue and numbers, enriching the diversity of the institution, or deepening the intellectual and cultural life of the campus. It is important that the institution be honest about its mission relative to the recruitment of international students. The market plan of an institution that wants primarily to diversify its population will be significantly different from that of an institution that wants primarily to increase revenue. Of course, the recruitment mission and goals must reflect and harmonize with the institution's overall mission.

The goals will identify the future direction of the recruitment effort based on whom the institution wants to recruit and what it wants its student population to look like in the future. For example, a predominantly undergraduate institution seeking to increase revenue could set as a goal the building of recognition and market in a region with few higher education opportunities coupled with a strong economic picture and a history of friendship with the United States. An intensive English program might target an emerging economy with growing foreign investment and an increased need for professionals who speak English. Goals in international student enrollment may be defined in terms of prosperity, favorable competitive position, institutional renown in certain fields or at certain levels of study, increasing enrollment or diversity, maintaining historical ties, developing new programs, or expanding the traditional campus mission.

Identification of Key Performance Indicators

Within the performance-based model of strategic planning, identifying key performance indicators plays a central role in strategic planning. A key performance indicator is a measure of an essential outcome of a particular organizational activity. It measures the outcomes of the various steps in the strategic planning process, and constantly checks performance against expectation. This performance measure ensures that the strategic plan remains practical. The plan itself should be specific, simple, and quantifiable. For example, a key performance indicator may be that 10 percent of the incoming class is international, or that the recruitment yield is the same as or higher than that of domestic students. Ensure that both quantitative measures, which are more easily identifiable, as well as more elusive but critically important qualitative measures are also included. The plan's success is judged by whether the specified outcome is realized. The selected indicators form a basic foundation for the strategic plan and ensure that the values, goals, action plan, and objectives are operational, measurable, and, above all, practical (Rowley, Lujan, and Dolence 1997; Dolence, Rowley, and Lujan 1997). These indicators also establish a metric for accountability, without which the plan will remain just a plan.

Identification of Objectives and Action Plan

Objectives that are identified within a strategic plan are considerably different from those in an operational plan. An operational plan, described in the next chapter, spells out how you are going to implement your strategic plan and might include specifics on staffing; budget recommendations; admission criteria; program acceptance; target countries; use of faculty, alumni, and students; and overseas contacts. Strategic objectives are less precise than operational ones and focus more on positioning than on specific accomplishments. They frequently identify where the planner wants to be at some point in the future—in international recruitment, the recommended timeline must be less than five years—and then work back to the present to plot the path to the goal. Marketing goals and target audiences must be prioritized. So, an undergraduate institution may decide to increase international enrollment in its allied health programs by 20 percent in five years, or a graduate program may decide to ensure that their engineering programs will be well known in the Middle East in three years. There should be a multiyear and a short-term plan, given the volatility of the international student market and global political and economic trends. Allow ample room for flexibility and creativity. Be realistic about your objectives. Make sure each one is feasible, measurable, and fits your strategic analysis, mission, and goals. Compare these to the key performance indicators identified earlier.

Accountability helps ensure that an action plan will be implemented. Plans are most effective if they are set on an annual basis. For example, you may decide to strengthen recruitment in one region and expand to two new regions each succeeding year. Timelines are developed, strategies are created, on- and off-campus infrastructure is outlined, and staff and resources are identified. An annual review and adjustment must be built-in to adjust strategies and review progress. That review will be more likely to remain up-to-date with swiftly changing global and regional trends if it includes information from sources used earlier in the external environmental scan, including colleagues in the same field of work. International education practitioners generally are collegial and generous with information and help.

Identification of Resources, Needs, and Expenditures

The systematic identification of needs and resources is often overlooked when planning an international recruitment strategy. Conduct an audit of resources currently used and resources that will be needed to support the strategic plan. Outline resource projections including technology for each part of the plan. This is also a time for research and advocacy. If you are able to show that the investment will meet and even exceed mission and revenue goals, your institution will be more likely to assign resources to this plan. Documented progress on key performance indicators will support future budgetary allocations for recruitment activities. Comparative information on the staffing and budgets of similar programs is also useful.

Budgets Should Include Allocations For:

- Staffing
- Postage and mailings
- Telephone, fax, and e-mail
- Web site
- Advertising

- Publications
- Travel
- Memberships and newsletters
- Reference library

Assessing Success

A sound strategic plan will produce successful enrollment and retention of international students. The danger is that the plan in isolation may become outdated quickly. Periodic evaluations of the recruiting plan and its impact on the campus environment can help an institution make mid-course corrections, such as adjusting outdated assumptions about the recruiting pool or reallocating resources from one service area to another based on student usage and demand. In an increasingly temperamental market, the plan has to be malleable and responsive. The administration must be informed and updated about international student flows so that the admission staff may be given the autonomy to make necessary adjustments to the plan.

Make sure that everyone who contributed to the process is acknowledged and receives a summary of the plan. Contributors should receive an executive summary annually. Solicit and incorporate feedback. Building ongoing support for the international recruitment effort is crucial to the success of the strategic plan. Student enrollments will quickly show you how effective your strategic plan is. The examples at the end of the chapter show three sample plans.

Finally, remember an international recruitment strategic plan is not a wish list or a marketing tool, nor should it be a solution for a problem facing the institution. It will be an invaluable tool to provide a blueprint for new direction and to shed light on a unique niche at the institution and ultimately contribute to a more globally educated population.

Bibliography

Bellow, Patrick J., George L. Morrisey, and Betty L. Acomb. 1987. *The Executive Guide to Strategic Planning.* San Francisco: Jossey-Bass.

Dolence, Michael G., Daniel James Rowley, and Herman D. Lujan. 1997. *Working Toward Strategic Change: A Step by Step Guide to the Planning Process.* San Francisco: Jossey-Bass.

Mind Tools. *Using the TOWS Matrix.* www.mindtools.com/pages/article/newSTR_89.htm. Accessed December 18, 2008.

Morrison, James L., 1992. "Environmental Scanning." In *A Primer for New Institutional Researchers,* eds. M. A. Whitely, J. A. Porter, and R. H. Fenske. Tallahasee, Florida: The Association for Institutional Research.

Rowley, Daniel James, Herman D. Lujan, and Michael G. Dolence. 1997. *Strategic Change in Colleges and Universities: Planning to Survive and Prosper.* San Francisco: Jossey-Bass.

Sevier, Robert A. 1996. "Those Important Things: What Every College President Needs to Know About Marketing and Student Recruiting," *College and University* 71, 4: 9-16.

Uhl, Norman P. 1983. "Institutional Research and Strategic Planning." In *Using Research for Strategic Planning,* ed. Norman P. Uhl. San Francisco: Jossey-Bass.

Wilkinson, R.B., James S. Taylor, Angé Peterson, and Maria de Lourdes Machado-Taylor, 2007. *A Practical Guide to Strategic Enrollment Management Planning in Higher Education.* Virginia Beach, VA: Educational Policy Institute

International Recruitment Strategic Plan Examples

Sample 1

SECTION A: Mission and Situational Analysis

1. Mission analysis

2. Situational analysis

3. Review of internal/institutional data

4. Review of external/environmental data

5. Compilation of strengths, weaknesses, opportunities, and threats

SECTION B: Marketing Goals and Audiences

1. Prioritized marketing goals

2. Prioritized target audiences

SECTION C: Strategies

1. Marketing action plans (including follow-up)

2. Budgets

3. Timelines

4. Mechanisms for evaluation

Sample 2

1. Select the initial planning committee.

2. Introduce the process.

3. Establish appropriate key performance indicators and organize key performance areas.

4. Survey the environment.

   - Assess external opportunities and threats.
   - Assess internal strengths and weaknesses.
   - Perform cross-impact analysis.

5. Share results with larger audience.

6. Develop definition and measurement criteria.

7. Measure current performance.

8. Establish two- and five-year goals.

9. Determine strategies in each area.

10. Establish broad-based support.

    - Develop appropriate polices for each key area.
    - Begin implementation process.
    - Measure performance frequently.
    - Perform one-year substantive review and modification.

Sample 3

Six-Phase Planning Process

Phase I:	Plan to Plan
Phase II:	Institutional Framework
Phase III:	SWOT
Phase IV:	Strategic Vision
Phase V:	Consensus Building
Phase VI:	Action

Adapted from Wilkinson, R.B., Taylor, James S., Peterson, Angé, and Machado-Taylor, Maria de Lourdes. 2007. *A Practical Guide to Strategic Enrollment Management Planning in Higher Education,* Education Policy Institute, available online at www.educationalpolicy.org/pdf/SEM%20Guide.pdf.

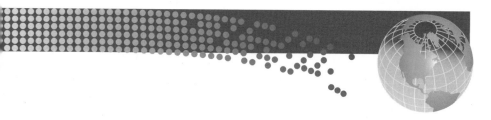

Writing the Annual Recruitment Plan

Sonja Phongsavanh

Writing the annual recruitment plan can be a daunting task, especially if you have not completed this mission previously. This chapter can assist you by demonstrating the process I have used in writing my institution's annual plan.

What Is an Annual Recruitment Plan?

The annual recruitment plan describes how the goals of the department's strategic plan will be met that year. It challenges the individuals working in the recruitment area to consider items such as budget, staffing, process, and procedures. How will they meet the department's objectives? Is there one person directly working with international recruitment? Ideally, that person should write the annual plan. If there is a team responsible for the task of international recruitment, then writing the plan should be a team effort.

Why Is It Important?

The annual recruitment plan serves three purposes. First, it acts as a roadmap for the office because it includes specific tasks and assignments along with dates, costs, and actual or projected outcomes. Second, it's an efficient way of showing other campus officials how your office is supporting departmental and institutional strategic planning efforts. Finally, the plan becomes a reliable record for your department and institution. You and your team will be able to refer to this written history for years to come.

Format

There is no required format for writing the annual recruitment plan. Use what you are most comfortable with, or what works for you and your institution.

Many institutions use an outline format that is easy for most individuals to write, share, and use. However, others add text, charts, and graphs to appeal to those wanting to see visual cues. Think about the persons on campus who will see the document. In some instances, who will see it will determine the layout of the document.

Reviewing the Data

Before writing the annual recruitment plan, you should review several items. First and foremost, examine the departmental strategic plan (see Chapter 2.2: Creating a Strategic Plan). Since the annual recruitment plan supports and is often viewed as a subset of the departmental strategic plan, it is important to be familiar with it and with your institutional strategic plan.

You also need to know how your institution fits with the rest of the world— that is against your institution's competitors in the United States as well as competitors from other countries. *Open Doors* and *Project Atlas,* both published by the Institute of International Education (www.iie.org), provide important information on student mobility and trends.

Next review the data from the past year (or years!) for international recruitment. If you are new to writing this document, you may not have sufficient data. You may need to interview others in your department to get the information you need. Do the best with what you have available. If this is your department's first international recruitment plan, know that you are establishing the groundwork for future planning efforts. Your work will be appreciated!

To determine the direction of your annual plan, ask yourself and your team several questions. What type of recruitment does your institution do? Travel? Armchair? Both? None? Did your institution travel in the past, and if so, where? What were the results? Can you build on recruitment efforts from previous years?

As you begin to ask and answer these questions, you need to examine and reflect to get the information. Consider this country-specific example:

- *Did you travel?* Yes

- *If so, where?* India

- *How many students did you meet?* 635

- *Did you receive applications?* Yes

- *If so*, how many? 320

- *How many were accepted?* 135

- *How many chose to deposit?* 88

From this example, you might infer that 88 new students from India were expected to arrive on campus in the fall. Is this number sufficient for you and your team to recommend another recruitment trip to India? Take another look at the information in this example. Consider the number of applications: 320. On some campuses this is a solid number of applications from one country, while at others it may not be. Is it for your campus? Only you and your team will be able to tell.

Now consider the number of applications that were accepted: 135, approximately 24 percent of the 320 applications received. Looking at this, you could interpret that the applications were not of sufficient quality to be accepted to your institution. Or it could mean that your institution did not receive all of the information from many of the applicants, and therefore a decision *could not* be made. Which was it? You need to look at additional reports, facts, and figures to have the complete picture. Once your picture is complete, you can make efficient use of your gathered information in writing your institution's annual plan.

Identifying Current Goals

Keep your institution's goals in mind while reviewing your institution's history and data. Are you trying to add diversity and/or increase the student body? Are you specifically tasked to recruit undergraduate students? Or graduate students? Knowing what you do about a particular country or region and its educational system, will that country be a good fit for your institution's goals? By keeping the answers to these questions and others like them in mind, you can better determine the best approach for your institution.

Identifying Recruitment Activities

As you consider writing your annual recruitment plan, think about the key recruitment activities such as advertising, travel, communication, etc. You may want to develop specific tasks for each of these activities and insert them into your annual recruitment plan in a particular section, or you may want to consider these individually as you think about your annual plan by country.

Continuing with India as an example, you could actually put into your annual plan a section specifically pertaining to India and ask the following questions:

1. *Travel:* Will you have someone travel to the particular country or will you utilize armchair recruiting methods?

2. *Communication:* How will you communicate with the population in this country? Will you send letters or e-mail to each group (e.g., inquiries, applicants)? Because India has a large population, is there more "bang for your buck" if you communicate only with applicants?

3. *Advertising:* Is it better to utilize print advertising in this market versus another region or country? Is online advertising better? Where does TV or radio fit into this plan?

4. *Alumni:* Is there an opportunity for alumni to give back to their alma mater by helping with recruitment initiatives? If so, how will you use them? Will they hold interviews? Work with a campus traveler in their city? Act as the main contact in an area? Organize and host events? If so, how will you determine who should represent your institution?

5. *Partnerships:* Will you be working with embassies and other organizations to recruit students from India? If so, how? Will you include them in travel initiatives in India or only visit their locations in the United States?

6. *Faculty:* What about using current faculty to meet your recruitment goals? And where do university agreements fit into the picture? Will your institution accept international transfers?

7. *Agents:* Will you consider utilizing agents in your recruitment plan? If so, how?

Now consider these same questions with China as the example; would your answers change? Change the example to Europe. Are the answers different? Do answers change because of the country or region or because of the population on your campus (e.g., large population, small population, undergraduate when you are interested in graduate)? There are more questions than on this list, and you will think of new ones as you write the plan. You will also find new answers to your questions in the weeks, months, and years to come.

The following is a template for subset plans/recruitment activities that I use when writing the annual plan. Keep in mind that you and your team will need to work to find the best solution for your institution. Although this template may not work for you, you may be able to utilize some of it so feel free to use what works for you.

Subset Plan/Activity List

Travel:

    Recruitment tours
    Independent travel with or
        without fairs

Communication groups:

    Fair/Event attendees
    Prospects
    Inquiries
    Applicants
    Accepted Students
    Deposited

Advertising:

    Web
    Print
    TV
    E-Mail

Partnerships:

    Universities
    Educational Advising Centers:
    Embassies and Agencies

In Country Presence:

    Alumni
    Faculty
    Agents
    Other

Allocating Resources

Once you have your thoughts on how you want to meet your goals, then it is time to think about allocating your resources including budget, time, and personnel. How will you accomplish all that you set out to do? Can one person do it? Are there others you can assign to the task? When you are assigning tasks, does anyone have a particular specialty in a certain area? Is there someone who speaks the language, is a national, has lived, traveled or studied in the country? Consider these issues when making travel assignments because it will make the work easier if there are already ties to the country.

Consider the time of year when the traveler(s) will be away. What is happening in the office? Is it a relatively slow period when more people can be out of the office, or would office productivity suffer? Timing is especially important if your office also has responsibility for domestic recruitment.

It is not uncommon for travelers to be away for weeks at a time, and in some instances months, depending on your institution and your plan. If travelers will be away for a significant length of time, is there someone in the office who can begin working with the contacts made on the road? Is the person traveling expected to maintain his or her own correspondence while they are on the other side of the world? How will other responsibilities, such as on-campus events, meeting students, and application processing, be handled while the traveler is away?

Include the cost for all of your recruitment activities in the budget. Although travel (shipping materials for the traveler, event registrations, advertising, airline costs, hotels, ground transportation, meals, etc.) will be a large part of your budget, you should also include the cost of items such as advertising, new publications, mailings, postage, and customer relationship management tools. For good decision-making, you need to have the full picture.

Making Adjustments

Suppose you developed the perfect plan for your institution, one that incorporated all of the items illustrated in this chapter. Then suppose you were told "your budget has to be cut by 15 percent and, by the way, we need to increase the international population on campus, especially students from XYZ country because a trustee and/or the president thinks this would be a good idea." Does this sound familiar? What do you do?

After the initial shock wears off, reconsider your plan. What are the essentials? What must be done to keep your international population from shrinking? Can you incorporate more armchair recruitment methods into your plan for a particular region or country? If not, is it possible to change your method of travel; small group or independent travel versus group travel? Would you consider taking large events such as fairs, with their significant costs, out of some of the areas? Would recruitment suffer?

And how does recruitment from XYZ country fit into your plan? Was it already considered? If so, does the plan need to change given that your budget has been reduced? If XYZ was not considered before, how will you begin your recruitment efforts there? Are there low-cost activities you can use such as talking with students from XYZ country already on your campus that you can begin conversations with? Are there current students that could begin some recruitment for you when they are in their home country during a break?

This example illustrates that things change and go awry even with the best annual plans. It does not have to be something on your campus or the whim of a trustee. Outside events beyond your control can (and do) skew your perfect plan, and you will need to make adjustments.

Using the Plan

Should the annual recruitment plan be written as a roadmap to your recruitment activities, or should it be written as a report that tells what you did throughout the year? Should it include projected budget figures or actual costs? Some institutions use the plan as a report on activities conducted throughout the year; others use it to predict what will happen; and some use it as a working document to review and update throughout the year. The advantage to the latter is that data can be taken from the plan to produce an annual report at the end of the year or recruitment cycle. This annual report can be very important in supporting your budget request for the following year.

In my own work, the annual recruitment plan is a working document. It is reviewed and discussed on a monthly basis. This document is also reviewed in conjunction with the strategic plan. Since the recruitment plan is a subset of the strategic plan, I want to see that the plans correlate, compliment each other, and advance the institution.

Coordinating with the Strategic Plan

As mentioned previously, the *departmental* strategic plan and the *institutional* strategic plan are important considerations when preparing the annual recruitment plan. The following is an example of a generic recruitment plan in action.

Institutional Goal: Increase the number of international students inquiring, applying for admission, and enrolling in graduate and undergraduate programs.

Departmental Goal: Become the preferred institutional choice for international students seeking academic preparation in the programs offered by the university.

Annual Plan: Conduct international recruitment travel and communicate with all students throughout the process. Travel will include college fairs, high school and university visits, information sessions and interviews for prospective students, meetings with counselors and agents, meetings with alumni and current students/parents.

a. Staff Travel
   i.   India: September Linden Tour (budget $17,000)
   ii. Asia: fall
      Select markets: South Korea, Taiwan, Malaysia, China, (budget $7,000)
   iii. Latin America: fall
      Select markets: Dominican Republic, Honduras, Peru, Colombia (budget $2600)
   iv. Europe: Spring 2006
      Select market: Turkey (budget $1500)
b. Faculty and Staff:
   i.   China
   ii. Europe
   iii. Caribbean
   iv. India (budget $2000)
c. Alumni
   i.   Cyprus: CIS Education Fair (budget $600)
   ii. Greece: CIS Education Fair (budget $600)
   iii. Istanbul: CIS Education Fair (budget $600)
   iv. Thailand: Assistance at education fair
   v. India: Assistance at education fair and school visits; spring accepted student presentations (budget $400)
   vi. China: Assistance at education fair, school visits

Departmental Goal: Alumni will play an increasingly prominent role in advancing the vision for student development and professional success.

Annual Plan: Develop specific plan for connecting with and involving international alumni in the recruitment process

a. Meet regularly with the alumni office on campus
b. Make connections and contact with alumni, and assist with implementation of outreach plan
c. Specific outreach in markets where there are particularly strong alumni

---

This example illustrates how you can incorporate the institutional and departmental strategic plans into your annual recruitment plan. By tying them together in one document, it will be easier for those outside your department to understand why you have chosen a particular activity; in this case travel to India.

Additionally, you may also use the subset plan/activity list as an appendix to this document. Feel free to use other appendixes if they work for you and your institution. It should be customized for you and your audience.

Stay Knowledgeable, Up-to-Date, and Flexible

There are a variety of items to be considered when writing the annual recruitment plan for your institution, and you may consider some or all of them. There may also be other items you will want to include, such as specific staff names or dates of recruitment events. An annual recruitment plan is not a "one-size-fits-all" solution because there are many factors to consider. The best plan spells out the work to be done, supports institutional and departmental goals, and becomes a history for future planning efforts. Those who know their institution well and keep up with what is happening in the field of international education and international recruitment are in the best position to write a useful and helpful plan.

Finally, the annual recruitment plan is not a static document, written once and executed. It will change as events happen and trends change. Economic changes, the events of September 11, SEVIS, and increased competition from other countries for international students are prime examples of events that have affected our recruitment plans. Each institution adapted in a different way, and you can be sure there will be more opportunities for U. S. institution's to show their flexibility in the future. Keep this in mind when preparing your annual recruitment plan...anything can happen.

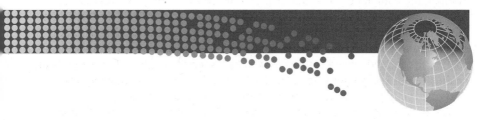

Building Foreign Credential Evaluation Expertise

Linda Jahn and Peggy Hendrickson

Building foreign credential evaluation expertise provides the international education specialist with endless opportunities for professional growth and development. With on-going changes in educational systems, credential evaluators will always face the challenge of finding information pertinent to the credentials before them. This chapter explores ways of building foreign credential evaluation expertise using NAFSA methodology.

Begin with U.S. Benchmarks

Understanding the U.S. educational system will provide the methodology for evaluating other educational systems. Elementary and secondary education are provided in 12 years (excluding kindergarten), with variations on how many grades are offered in the different types of schools within each school district. Upon completion of the 12-year system, when all requirements have been met, the student is awarded the high school diploma. Depending on the high school curriculum followed, the student with the high school diploma can choose to attend a university, college, community college, vocational institute, or enter the workforce. We call the high school diploma a benchmark credential because it marks the point of completion of one level of education and provides access to another level.

The next level in the U.S. educational system is the postsecondary level. If the student continues studying at the college/university level, there are other benchmark credentials to be earned upon completion of required credits and years of study. The associate degree usually is awarded upon completion of two years of postsecondary study or 66 semester hours of credit (90 plus quarter hours) with required subjects. With the associate degree, a student can go from a community/junior college to a four-year college or university. Students can also transfer to colleges and universities without the associate degree; however, the associate degree marks the end of a specific two-year degree program.

At the university level, the bachelor's degree is the first benchmark credential, marking the completion of a four-year or 120-semester hour/180-quarter hour (minimum) prescribed program in a specific field of study. This degree requires a high school diploma for entry, and it includes both general education requirements and a specified number of major credits in a progression from introductory courses to more advanced courses as well as a specific number of upper division credits (junior and senior level). The bachelor's degree usually provides access to study for the master's degree (and sometimes doctorate) studies.

The master's degree is usually awarded after one to two years of full-time graduate level study (30 semester hours/45 quarter hours), completing required advanced studies in a major field and possibly some core courses.

The doctorate (doctor of philosophy) usually requires a bachelor's degree or master's degree for admission. It is the highest academic degree granted by U.S. universities, and it includes a significant period of study with a faculty mentor and course work plus a dissertation written upon completion of extensive research. Other doctoral degrees such as the juris doctor, doctor of medicine, doctor of education, doctor of dental surgery, etc. provide applied advanced training within a professional field of study.

This is a brief description of the benchmark credentials in the U.S. educational system. The foreign credential evaluation expert will review the educational systems of other countries for benchmark credentials comparable to those of the United States. The basic questions to ask are:

1. What level of education does the foreign credential represent, and what were the entrance requirements? Is this comparable to a U.S. benchmark?

2. Does the program leading to the credential include the same number of years of study and comparable course content as the U.S. benchmark credential?

3. Does it give access in the home country to the same higher level of study as the U.S. benchmark credential?

If the answer is yes, you can decide to admit the student at the appropriate level of program based on grades earned. If the answer is no, you may decide that the student is qualified for admission to another program at your institution or you may deny admission to your institution.

Authenticity of Credentials

Another important step in evaluating foreign educational records is determining the authenticity of the credential. In the United States, most credentials issued by school systems or institutions are uniform in appearance. An individual school or the school district usually issues the elementary and secondary school credentials. At the college/university level, individual institutions have the authority to award degrees and issue official transcripts and degree certificates. In other countries, a board of examinations, the ministry of education, secretary of education, the individual school, a regional authority, a qualifications commission, or many other official bodies may issue official records. The foreign credential evaluator must learn what sources in each country are the official, recognized bodies with the authority to issue educational credentials.

Check the Web site of the ministry of education/ministry of higher education for each country (see Appendix B: Ministries of Education by Country). Also, use the NAFSA Recruitment, Admissions, and Preparation Knowledge Community (www.nafsa.org/RAP) for research in educational systems and institutions.

After learning about the authenticating body, you may determine that the credentials came to you directly from the issuing source and did not pass through the student's hands. If so, you may proceed to review the document for other authenticating factors. Or, if the document did not come directly to you from the issuing office, you may want to verify the documents by sending photocopies of them back to the original source with a letter requesting verification of their authenticity.

Questions you should ask to help determine the authenticity of records:

- Is the document on official letterhead and did it arrive in your office directly from the issuing body? If the issuing body creates only one original, are the photocopies authenticated/attested by the appropriate school official after being photocopied?

- Does the document have the appropriate official signature and seal?

- Does the document specify the location (city, country) of issue?

- Does the document appear in the normal format for similar records issued by that authority? Check with the American Association of Collegiate Registrars and Admissions Officers (AACRAO, www.aacrao.org) and with NAFSA for publications that show sample credentials in correct format.

- Does the document contain spelling errors or typos?

- Does the student's name appear on all pages of the record?

- Does the student's identification information on the document match what the student wrote on his/her application to your institution? (Date of birth, location of birth, years of attendance, etc.)

- Was the student the appropriate age when the credential was awarded?

- Are there smudge marks, erasures or white-out on the document?

- Do you have an authentic document in the original language of the issuing country as well as a certified English translation? Beware of literal translations such as "baccalaureate" translated as a bachelor's degree and other interpretations made by the translator.

Accreditation As Opposed to Recognition

In the United States, public elementary and secondary schools report to independent school districts and require students to meet specific state requirements for advancement to the next grade or for graduation. Private schools are usually autonomous and determine their own requirements for advancement/graduation; however, they may choose to follow the state requirements specified for public schools.

Because the United States has no national body governing colleges and universities, nongovernmental, private regional accreditation associations are responsible for the review and accreditation of such institutions. A college or university may choose to apply to a regional association for accreditation and will undergo a long review process before accreditation is granted. Each regional association has its own criteria for accreditation; however, all six regional accreditations are considered equal.

While the institution is under review by one of the regional accreditation associations, it is said to be in "candidate" status. Once accreditation is granted, the institution may identify itself as accredited by the regional accreditation association. To check the accreditation status of a college or university, go to the Web site of the association by first looking at the Council for Higher Education Accreditation site, www.chea.org, or see the publication *Transfer Credit Practices of Designated Educational Institution,* published by AACRAO.

Another excellent source of information on legitimate accreditation as opposed to accreditation mills and diploma mills is *Accreditation Mills,* published by AACRAO.

Unlike the U.S. accreditation system, most countries have a national ministry of education and/or a ministry of higher education that oversees education and "recognizes" institutions and credentials within the country. The ministry of education/higher education usually sets standards for education that must be met for institutions at each level of education to be "recognized" by the ministry. The foreign credential evaluator must determine how the ministry of education/higher education or accrediting body recognizes specific institutions, programs, and credentials and then must determine the comparability of that within the U.S. educational system.

Does the ministry of education recognize a specific credential at the primary or secondary school level? Or is the credential awarded at the university level? Does the ministry of education recognize the body/institution that awards the credential? NAFSA and AACRAO resources on specific countries or groups of countries include much of this information. Please see the section Databases and Listservs as well as Appendix B, Ministries of Education by Country.

Simply because an institution has been given the legal authority to exist within a specific country does not automatically mean that it is *recognized* by the ministry of education. In most countries, institutions wanting to operate must apply to the government or ministry of education for permission to open. If the government grants an institution the authority to exist, it may deem the institution as "incorporated, chartered, licensed, or registered." These terms, however, do **not** automatically mean that the government recognizes the institution and grants it the authority to award specific degrees/diplomas or to offer the level of programs it does consider "accredited" or "recognized." The question to ask is "At what level (if any) does the ministry of education recognize the institution, academic program, and credentials in question?"

Some specialized programs are given recognition by a ministry other than the ministry of education; for example, the ministry of health, ministry of agriculture, ministry of social services, or a national vocational education authority. It is the responsibility of the international credential evaluator to learn how the specific program compares with U.S. programs in that field of study and what the program gives access to in the home country. This will assist the evaluator in determining U.S. comparability.

If you have determined that a credential is authentic, that the institution issuing it is recognized (and specific level of recognition), that it represents education comparable to a U.S. benchmark credential, and that it has been issued by the appropriate authority for the specific country of issue, you can continue with the evaluation of the document.

Grading

In the United States, most schools use a letter system of grading (A through F) with a four-point scale of passing grades.

Excellent:	A + /A/A-
Good:	B + /B/B-
Average:	C + /C/C-
Below Average:	D + /D/D-
Failure	F

The minimum grade required to obtain a benchmark credential in the U.S. is:

High School:	D/1.00 average on a 4.00 scale
Undergraduate Level:	C/2.00 average on a 4.00 scale
Graduate Level:	B/3.00 average on a 4.00 scale

In other countries, the grading scale may be numeric with specific minimum and maximum scores, percentage grading not similar to the U.S. letter grading other than A–F, pass/fail, good/pass/fail, and many others. Grading scales may vary within one country, from institution to institution, by level of educational program, and numerous other factors. Use available resources to determine the grading scale for each document in question.

Printed Resources

General and Multicountry

Commonwealth Universities Yearbook. Information on universities within the British Commonwealth. www.palgraves.com

International Handbook of Universities. Information on recognized universities throughout the world. www.palgraves.com

Guide to Educational Systems Around the World. Information on educational systems, credentials, and grading information for many countries. www.nafsa.org/epubs

World of Learning. Information on educational institutions around the world. www.europapublications.co.uk

The New Country Index. Information on educational systems and credentials, with placement recommendations for a wide range of countries. www.ierf.org

Foreign Educational Credentials Required. Information on credentials and other documentation required for entry from a given country to a specified level of study. www.aacrao.org

Guide to Bogus Institutions and Documents. Information on problem of bogus universities and degree fraud, bogus institutions and documents, and offers guidelines in handling cases of fraud. www.aacrao.org

Country-Specific and Multicountry

Country-specific resources usually provide an overview of the educational system of the country, curriculum information, grading scales, placement recommendations, and other valuable information.

Multicountry resources provide information about education in specific regions of the world, the similarities and differences between countries within the region, governmental theories and approaches to education, structure of educational system, curricula, grading, levels of education, policies, credentials issued, and much more.

British Qualifications. Information on education within the United Kingdom, including specific institutions and professional associations that provide training. www.kogan-page.co.uk

National Office of Overseas Skills Recognition (NOOSR) series of country studies provides information from the Australian educational perspective regarding other countries' educational systems. http://aei.dest.gov.au/AEI/Default.html

Guide to Higher Education in Africa. Contains details on the educational systems, their institutions, and the national education authority for each of 47 African countries. www.unesco.org/iau/directories/guide.html

World List of Universities and Other Institutions of Higher Education. Provides data on universities and other institutions specifically offering terminal degrees after three to four years of higher education worldwide. www.unesco.org/iau/directories/worldlist.html

Free: *Country Higher Education Profiles.* International network for higher education in Africa. www.bc.edu/bc_org/avp/soe/cihe/inhea/profiles.htm

Free: *World Education Profiles.* World Education Services, www.wes.org/ca/wedb/ecountrylist.htm

Databases and Listservs

The World Academic Database includes descriptions of educational systems and a listing of recognized universities for each country in the database. www.unesco.org/iau/onlinedatabases/index.html

The ENIC-NARIC network provides country profiles and updates on the Bologna Agreement (ENIC: The European Network of Information Centres) (NARIC: National Academic Recognition Information Centres). www.enic-naric.net/

Eurydice Information Network on Education in Europe provides a database known as Eurybase of educational systems in Europe. http://eacea.ec.europa.eu/portal/page/portal/Eurydice

AACRAO Electronic Database for Global Education (EDGE) is a Web-based subscription resource for evaluating foreign educational credentials. www.aacraoedge.aacrao.org/register/

Be sure to check your local, state, and regional areas for similar groups in your particular area of the country.

Inter-l: inter-l@yahoogroups.com

AMIE: AMIE_list@yahoogroups.com

NAFSA Knowledge Communities: www.nafsa.org/networks

TACRAO: tacrao@listserv.utpa.edu (sign up: tacrao-subscribe-request@listserv.utpa.edu)

Texas Higher Education List-serve: the-l@listserv.uhd.edu

One-Way Mailing Lists/Newsletter

- NAFSA Region III newsletter: www.nafsa3.org

- ECE mailing newsletter:
  http://lists.lyris.net/cgi-bin/lists.pl?enter = ece-newsletter

- AMIDEAST newsletter:
  www.amideast.org/whats_new/ae_newsletter/default.htm

- British Council newsletter: educationuk-l@britishcouncil.org

- DAAD German Academic Exchange Service newsletter:
  www.daad.org/?p = 46367#newsletters

- Association of African Universities E-courier:
  www.aau.org/elists/listinfo/aau-ecourier

- International Association of Universities e-bulletin:
  www.aau.org/e-courier/index.htm

Media Resources

In addition to international newspapers and magazines, and international news broadcasts such as CNN and BBC:

- ECE Newsletter: www.ece.org

- NAFSA.news: www.nafsa.org

- World Education News and Reviews (WENR): www.wes.org

- wRAP-UP Newsletter: www.nafsa.org

- European Association of International Educators (EAIE), see section for Admissions officers and credential evaluators: www.eaie.org/ACE/

- *The Chronicle of Higher Education*

- *International Educator magazine:* www.nafsa.org/ie

- Inside Higher Ed: www.insidehighered.com/

- Institute for Higher Education Policy: www.ihep.org/

Country Files

Create your own filing system. Information collected regarding country educational systems, credentials, grading scales, etc. can be archived in a specific country file for each country. These can be paper files and also virtual files. Save e-mail messages and written responses to your inquiries.

Workshop Materials

NAFSA, AACRAO, and EAIE offer workshops for foreign credential evaluators at annual and regional conferences, as well as on-demand. Become a member of these associations and take advantage of a member discount to attend these training sessions. Networking among these organizations is a key to developing contacts with colleagues who have expertise in numerous areas of international education.

- NAFSA: Association of International Educators

- AACRAO: American Association of Collegiate Registrars and Admissions Officers

- EAIE: European Association of International Educators

Get to Know the OSEAS Advisers

EducationUSA offices around the world have advisers who assist students coming from other countries to the United States. These advisers are members of NAFSA and you can meet them at annual and regional conferences. Contact them by e-mail for information on specific credentials, education system information, and help with records from specific institutions within their country. They are an excellent link to information you need to do your job well! (www.educationusa. state.gov/centers.htm)

Develop Expertise Through Research

There's nothing like diving in on your own and doing your own research. After all, this is what international credential evaluation is about. Select a country, review the Web site of the ministry of education, read all you can find about the educational system, credentials, and grading. Call the embassy for that country and ask questions of the educational attaché. Review periodicals for current changes to the educational system. Watch the various news broadcasts, including international and U.S. channels. Get different perspectives on the country's education. And remember, education in one country isn't necessarily better or worse than in another country. It's just different, so learn about it and see how it fits into the educational programs at your institution for students wanting to come and study. International students will enhance education on your campus if they are treated fairly by someone who is knowledgeable about their credentials.

If you don't know the answers immediately, offer to take some time to check before you make your decisions and do additional research. Call colleagues at other schools to learn how they have handled similar credentials so that you don't have to reinvent the wheel.

A good rule to follow is: One year of education in any country equals one year of education in another country. You wouldn't give a student in Iowa more credit per year than you would a student from Texas. The time in the classroom, laboratory facilities, library resources, time for individual study, and many other factors will vary from country to country. But in one academic year, a full-time student in one country will have completed education comparable to a full-time student in any other country. Don't try to justify whose education is better. It's simply a matter of what's realistically possible, and it will spare you from having to debate with students.

So, get ready for the ride of a lifetime and a profession that will enrich your life in ways you never imagined!

The Pros and Cons of Using Credential Evaluation Companies

Choosing a private evaluation company can be a stressful experience because each company has its own criteria, equivalencies, grading scales, and other methodologies. They also have different goals than do educational institutions in that they provide evaluations for professional licensing, employment, immigration, as well as educational purposes.

Regarding private evaluation companies, an excellent place to start would be with the members of the Association of International Credentials Evaluators (AICE) or the National Association of Credential Evaluation Services (NACES), two private associations that have membership requirements, codes of ethics, and high standards. Institutions and students using these affiliated credentials evaluation companies should be able to readily determine that the agency they select is not a fly-by-night company with little to no training or experience in the field.

In addition, NAFSA offers a practice resource, A Guide to Selecting a Foreign Credentials Evaluation Service, that has a series of questions institutions can ask when choosing an international credentials agency: www.nafsa.org/knowledge_community_network.sec/recruitment_admissions/admissions_and_credential/practice_resources_19.

When using a company for the first time, one strategy would be to contact NAFSA Region members where that agency is located to see if the local international education community can offer their opinion: www.nafsa.org/nafsa_regions.sec. Please note that, sometimes, private companies choose not to be members of one of the above agencies for their own reasons and not because they are lacking in any quality or expertise.

As an example, there are several reputable private evaluation firms throughout Texas that may or may not have membership in NACES or AICE but are very active in the international education community by presenting, publishing, and volunteering regularly throughout the state and region. As such, credentials evaluation members of the Region III Team may be able to offer an informed opinion about the experience and expertise of a private evaluation company, regardless of its membership.

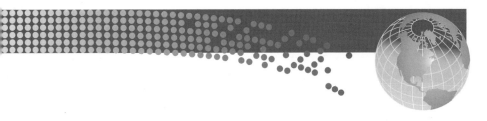

International Student and Exchange Visitor Visas in a Post-September 11 World

Marjory Gooding

Any discussion of ethical recruitment in a post-September 11 world must include mention of the legal environment in which international students and scholars come to the United States. The popular press made much of the fact that one of the 9/11 terrorists entered to the United States on a student visa. Government regulators picked up on this and reacted with predictable actions, largely because international students were an identifiable population that was already being tracked by colleges and universities under then-existing regulations.

The result was a climate of fear on both sides of the exchange equation. That fear now manifests itself in visa acquisition procedures, immigration regulations, and electronic tracking systems. While the panic has somewhat died down, inbound students still have many questions about whether they will be able to get the visa once they are admitted to a U.S. institution. They are also anxious about whether they will be able to travel home once they are studying in the United States. Their parents, meanwhile, may have completely different concerns about their student's safety in the United States.

Being able to give good answers requires having background information about the U.S. government agencies involved in the process, knowledge about U.S. immigration regulations, and a good referral system to the advisers in the international office on campus. For starters, the Immigration and Naturalization Service (INS) was replaced by a much larger agency called the Department of Homeland Security (DHS). DHS works with international students once they are inside the United States, while the U.S. Department of State works with them when they are outside the United States, e.g., when they are applying for visas.

So Many Questions!

Some good, short answers to a few of those questions:

- Thousands of international students and exchange visitors succeed in getting their U.S. visas every year.

- International students occasionally run into problems in the visa acquisition process, but this is the exception rather than the rule.

- International students occasionally run into problems with the immigration system while in the United States, but this is the exception rather than the rule.

- International students occasionally run into problems with international travel during the time they are studying in the United States, but this is the exception rather than the rule.

- The international office on campus is the best source of information (much better than your cousin).

- Visa fees and tracking fees are somewhat expensive. However, at least part of this is based on reciprocity among countries.

- There is a tracking system known as the Student and Exchange Visitor Information System or SEVIS. It is a complicated system with many technical challenges. It is designed to track international students from the time initial immigration documents are issued through the time that the student finally leaves the United States.

- It is important to know that the data in the various data systems of the U.S. government is not necessarily synchronized. This knowledge helps international students understand some of the problems that do arise.

- Work options for international students do exist, but they are complicated. It is very helpful to refer students to the international office for the latest information.

What Are the Numbers?

There are many ways of counting how many international students and exchange visitors are currently in the United States. One good source is *Open Doors*, published by the Institute for International Education (IIE), which is widely seen as the most reliable compilation of information about student and scholar mobility. Another source of information is the U.S. government tracking system (SEVIS). As of April 15, 2008, this system indicated that there are 672,030 F-1 students in the United States and 241,113 exchange visitors in the United States. The numbers presented in *Open Doors* are a university-based snapshot picture and do not include many of the categories used outside academe. For this reason the two sources may not line up, but these numbers give you some sense of the scope of mobility of international students and scholars coming to the United States.

What Happens When

These are the steps an international student must take to study in the United States:

- Applies to and is admitted to a U.S. college or university, after demonstrating appropriate academic preparation, linguistic readiness, and financial means.

- Receives government forms (I-20 for most students; DS 2019 for exchange visitors) prepared by the international office at the accepting college or university.

- Pays the SEVIS fee online, as well as a visa reciprocity fee, if appropriate. The visa reciprocity fee is usually paid at a bank near the U.S. consulate.

- Arranges for an interview for an F-1 or J-1 visa at the appropriate U.S. consulate (part of the U.S. Department of State) that has jurisdiction over his/her place of residence. In addition to academic, linguistic, and financial readiness, the student must also demonstrate that he/she has adequate ties to his/her home country and that he/she intends to return there after completing their studies.

- Obtains the F-1 or J-1 visa.

- Travels to the United States.

- Goes through "inspection" at the port of entry by officials of the Department of Homeland Security (DHS). If all documents and records are in order, the student is "admitted" to the United States.

- Checks in with the international office at the university. The international office does an appropriate electronic "validation" of the individual's SEVIS record.

How long does all this take? It may be as short as a few days, but it is more likely that the entire process will take two to three months after acceptance. Students must make an application for a visa interview, generally done online or by phone. The wait for an interview may last several weeks, particularly during the summer months when other U.S.-bound students are making similar applications. Students should be referred to the international office and to www.travel.state.gov/.

Basic Assumptions in Immigration Law

Recruiters can help incoming students sort fact-from-fiction by becoming acquainted with some of the basic concepts in immigration law. It is not necessary to be an expert in this field, but it is helpful to understand some of the basic premises. This is the best way to help students who run into unforeseen obstacles.

- People coming to the United States temporarily are called "nonimmigrants" and people coming to the United States permanently are called "immigrants." This distinction seems so simple, but many other ideas spring from this dichotomy.

- People coming to the United States are assumed by the consular officer (official at the U.S. consulate who grants visas) to be "intending immigrants" unless they can prove otherwise. Incoming students in both F-1 and J-1 status must be able to demonstrate that they are not "intending immigrants" and that they will return home after they complete their studies. The key factors that U.S. consular officers consider are:

  - The ties to one's home country

  - Any family remaining in the home country

  - Logical career paths in the home country

  - Adequate preparation for the planned course of study

  - Financing that makes sense and is sustainable.

- Nonimmigrants come to the United States for a wide variety of purposes. They may come as tourists, visitors for business, to study, to conduct research, to perform, to consult, etc. The letters and numbers associated with various nonimmigrant classifications reflect the paragraphs in the Immigration and Nationality Act (INA), which is the basic U.S. immigration statute. The letters and numbers don't have meaning other than that. The paragraph in the INA that creates student status is paragraph F; the paragraph in the INA that creates exchange visitor status is paragraph J. The number "1" refers to the principal applicant; the number "2" usually refers to the dependents of the principal.

- When an incoming student signs his/her immigration documents, he/she accepts all the terms and conditions of the status. In very general terms, this means that the incoming student agrees to come for the appropriate purpose, to leave the United States when he/she completes studies, and that he/she understands that various privacy rights are waived. The student agrees to keep the government informed of his/her address changes. The enrolling school agrees to keep the government informed of the students' academic status, contact information, course of study, term-by-term enrollment, full-course of study, and completion of degree. This reporting happens electronically through the SEVIS system.

- Immigration law and labor law are designed to protect U.S. jobs for U.S. citizens, unless exceptions are specifically called out in the regulations. International students can only work under specific conditions. In very general terms, F-1 students can work part-time on campus or take assistantships, and can secure a period of "practical training" in their field once they have graduated. The regulations surrounding employment in the United States are exceedingly complex. Incoming students should be referred to their international office for details.

Helpful Terminology

Immigration regulations are full of special terms. Some of these are important for recruiters because incoming students have so many questions about the immigration process.

Visa. The U.S. visa is the stamp placed by a U.S. consular officer (an employee of the U.S. Department of State) on a page in the student's passport during the visa interview. The term "visa" is frequently used incorrectly to mean one's legal status and/or permission to remain in the United States. In fact, it has a narrower and more limited meaning. It only indicates that a consular officer has determined that the holder is qualified to ask for entry to the United States at a port of entry. The final decision to "admit" the person to the United States is made by the official at the port of entry who inspects the passport, the visa, and the underlying documents. Visas have their own expiration dates. These expiration dates may or may not match the length of time that the student intends to study in the United States. The validity period of the visa is based on reciprocity agreements that exist between the United States and all other countries. Thus, the visa may be valid for only a few months, whereas the student may be coming to study for years. The visa needs to be valid only when the student comes to the U.S. port of entry from outside the United States.

I-20. This is the document prepared through SEVIS by the international office at the accepting university if the student is coming in the usual manner, i.e., in F-1 status. The I-20 attests to the fact that the student has been deemed academically, financially, and linguistically qualified to attend the university. It also details the projected costs, resources, accompanying family members, and other pertinent information. These seem like simple documents; they are not. The advisers in the international office are the best source of information on the details.

DS 2019. This is the document prepared through SEVIS by the international office at the accepting university or other agency if the student is coming as an "exchange visitor" in J-1 status. Similar to an I-20, the DS 2019 contains a great deal of information. Why the distinction? Exchange visitor programs enable many categories beyond just the student category. These include researchers, professors, au pair placements, camp counselor positions, trainee programs, and secondary teachers, among others. These programs are administered by the Exchange Visitor Program that is part of the Bureau of Educational and Cultural Affairs within the Department of State. Not surprisingly, J-1 status has very different regulations from F-1 status. Again, it is important to refer inbound students to the international office for details.

Designated School Official or Responsible Officer. These are terms that refer to individuals at the accepting university who are specifically charged by DHS or the Department of State with the responsibilities of carrying out all the appropriate advising and reporting that goes along with the university's ability to enroll international students. Many people take it for granted that it is the right of a university to enroll internationals because this has been our practice for so many decades. In fact, the processes for "certification" or "designation" are complex and involve many steps. Most U.S. universities have both F and J programs. Many smaller institutions enroll only F students, leaving the more complicated J programs aside.

Green Card. There are lots of misconceptions about this. It's the popular term for the card that an individual receives when he/she becomes a legal permanent resident, or resident alien, of the United States. The other term for such individuals is "immigrant." As you can readily see, this term is often used incorrectly in the press, which leads to much of the confusion. Sometimes incoming students wonder why they should bother with a "nonimmigrant" status—they hope that they can simply be sponsored for a green card and bypass all the nonimmigrant regulations. In fact, that's much more complicated than they might expect. There is good information about the various pathways to permanent residency on the DHS Web site, www.uscis.gov/portal/site/uscis.

SEVIS. The "Student and Exchange Visitor Information System" is the database managed by the U.S. Department of Homeland Security, used to monitor student and exchange visitor activity and facilitate compliance with student and exchange visitor regulations.

NAFSA Immigration Resources

NAFSA publishes a variety of materials that help international education professionals work effectively with DHS regulations governing international students and scholars studying in the United States.

- *NAFSA Adviser's Manual Online,* edited by David Fosnocht. This is the adviser's standard reference work on immigration law and procedure affecting colleges and universities. It is accessible in electronic form by subscription.

- *Immigration Classifications and Legal Employment of Foreign Nationals in the United States,* 2008, edited by Gail Rawson. This is a periodically updated poster-size chart that describes each immigrant and nonimmigrant classification, provides information on employment eligibility and study options, and explains the documentation required in each case.

Please see www.nafsa.org/publications for additional publication information.

Please note that NAFSA also offers an extensive curriculum on regulatory matters for international educators. People involved in recruitment may want to take the one-day "F-1 for Beginners" workshop as a foundation on which to build their knowledge and skills. This workshop is offered at most NAFSA conferences as well as in stand-alone venues. NAFSA also offers online training. Please visit www.nafsa.org/events.sec for more opportunities.

Recruitment Techniques

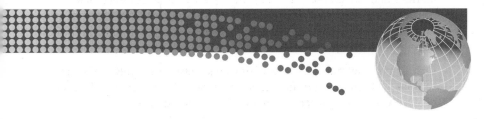

Advertising: What, Where, and When to Say It

Peggy J. Printz

● ● ● ●

Good advertising does not just circulate information. It penetrates the public mind with desires and belief.

—*Leo Burnett, advertising guru*

Advertising can be extremely effective in reaching audiences who have little or no familiarity with your program. Even when you travel, it's still vital to supplement your personal contacts with print and Internet promotion, alumni contacts, and other proactive projects. An effective advertising effort requires careful planning, hard work, and communication—on and off campus, domestically, and internationally. Although advertising may be easier on you, and on the planet, than international travel, it nevertheless requires some investment in time and money.

What are the advantages for you to advertise when recruiting international students?

- *Relatively inexpensive.* It is when compared to traveling the world or using agents. Mailing brochures and promoting your Web site expands your global presence while newspaper advertising focuses on certain populations. You can leverage small sums into greater exposure by advertising in a recruitment publication, directory, or Web site.

- *Efficient.* Advertising condenses your message into a tidy, user-friendly format. Within a confined space, you must convey your institution's distinctive features to remote strangers. As a result, you are forced to directly and concisely define your program's differential advantages.

- *Specific Focus.* Through well-placed ads, you can reach your desired markets and age groups. Most international recruitment directories are distributed in countries where the students can obtain visas and can afford to study abroad. Some guidebooks and Web sites are translated into foreign languages, making them user-friendly to parents and spouses.

- *Convenient.* You purchase advertising space from the comfort of your campus, without concern for tickets, reservations, and jetlag. Advertising enables you to be "present" in many time zones at once.

- *Flexible.* You can use a variety of channels: online and print (magazines, brochures, posters, mailings, local ethnic newspapers).

- *Effective.* Advertising provides a fun, eye-catching means to create awareness of your institution or program among your intended customers.

What to Say

Advertising conveys *image* rather than *substance,* so give careful consideration to the impression you wish to project. Find your focus. What makes your institution unique? What factors motivate students to apply there?

Identify your comparative advantages, such as:

- Your institution's reputation

- Popular courses of study, i.e. architecture, computer science, business administration, travel industry management

- Campus location

- Low cost, good value

Stress your academic strengths, such as "Learn English and Earn a Degree in Sunny Southern California" or "Your Art Career Begins Here!" Or other factors, such as "Quality, Affordable Education," or "A Safe, Friendly Campus."

Identify Your Audience

Where—in what countries or regions—do you want to concentrate your advertising dollars? This is a decision that you and your colleagues will want to revisit periodically.

You may decide to focus on specific areas of the world where demographics match your institution's profile. Schools in the Southeast, for example, or Roman Catholic universities, may find good markets in central and South America; programs in the western United States could look toward Asia because of lower travel costs. Conversely, to diversify student enrollment you can pinpoint areas for recruitment where your campus population is underrepresented. The strengths you highlight might differ depending on your location. Applicants from Japan will seek out a small-town environment where there are few other Japanese students, and they will be obliged to speak English consistently. But students from the Middle East may find urban locations preferable because of their proximity to mosques or synagogues.

What Students Want to Know About Your Institution

- Course of study
- Popular majors (with international students)
- Location (spell out state name)
- Degrees offered
- Short-term and summer programs
- ESL and intensive English classes
- Conditional admission, if relevant

- Services, especially airport pick-up
- Residence halls
- Help finding housing
- Homestays
- Prayer facilities
- Safety
- Recreation

Meshing with Your Marketing Plan

In an ideal situation, you can synchronize your publicity with campus-wide efforts and economize on advertising costs by working with your campus design and marketing team.

In trying to conform to campus-wide "branding" standards, or to save money, however, do not be tempted to use domestic recruitment material for international initiatives. Messages you would normally send to U.S. students can backfire when received overseas. Or, they may simply fall flat. Such is often the case with American idioms, for example, "You can get there from here." Students in Venezuela or Vietnam won't understand the pun and could be just plain confused by it.

Likewise, well-meaning slogans such as "A World of Difference," may be irrelevant or incomprehensible to students who are already "multicultural." These young people are not seeking diversity but want to experience U.S. academic excellence and meet Americans.

Translation

Why translate? Doesn't everyone read English? Won't students think they can attend your university without learning English? Doesn't it take a lot of time and money to have material translated? Translating your marketing material does not indicate that you accept students who speak only their native languages or have a low level of English comprehension. It does mean that students, parents, and spouses are *far more likely to read your information.*

Translating can be time consuming because you need to find reliable translators, and even then you must proofread carefully. And please, always use a proofreader who is a native speaker. This true story relates why. One of the online ads at a U.S. admissions publisher intended to say: "Come study in the U.S.A. at an excellent institution," but it came back from a respected Spanish translator as: "Come to the U.S.A. and be institutionalized"! Fortunately, proofreading caught the mistake.

Updating translated text can be a chore, especially on the Web. So, consider participating in services and directories that manage translation for you—the translated materials reside on their sites, and students can conveniently click there from buttons on your home page. Use HTML formatting rather than PDF to display translated text on your site. Viewing a PDF sometimes requires a download and thus places a barrier between your information and the students reading it. Also, PDF files are generally read-only and don't have the interaction to let students request information electronically. HTML, on the other hand, is searchable and easier to see at a glance.

Finding someone who can translate *and* format for the Internet can be a challenge but is worth the effort. And if you are concerned about having to translate requests for information, you can always ask students, "Please respond in English."

Where to Say It

You have many appealing alternatives: you can concentrate on do-it-yourself formats such as posters and brochures; you can enhance your university Web site to make it a magnet for visitors; and you can join directories and magazines, local and international newspapers, or admissions Web sites. It may be advantageous to utilize both print and electronic media as you identify the markets suited to your institution.

How do you break into advertising overseas? How do you know which publications and Internet services are legitimate and will actually reach your intended audience? Follow the footsteps of your NAFSA colleagues and use reputable services by referring to the Checklist: What to Consider Before You Advertise.

Internet and Electronic Media

Before you start advertising to drive traffic to your Web site, make it a user-friendly resource for international visitors. Follow the fundamentals of good site design: lead with your best advantage, standardize your navigation buttons, use short screens (1-1/4 pages maximum), and funnel traffic to a destination: your enrollment application! You can find useful tips at: http://educationusa.state.gov/home/education/intl_web.htm.

Naturally you will want to take advantage of the normal methods of search engine optimization—embedding your school's name in HTML coding, buying search terms such as "American education" or "Study in Massachusetts," etc. Purchasing advertising generated by key terms on the major search engines can be very expensive. Therefore, many institutions use large admissions sites or directories and benefit from the prominent search engine exposure they enjoy. Some of these sites specialize in a certain level of education, such as M.B.A. guidebooks, or location—studying in the United States or Canada. When choosing a directory, search for and visit the site as a prospective international student so that you can determine its "usability." Discover for yourself which sites are listed highest on the screen and then which are easiest to navigate.

What to Consider Before You Advertise

REPUTATION

- What is the publication/Web site's reputation and track record?

- How long has it been in existence?

- How many previous participants renew each year?

- Ask for references. Ask your colleagues about their experience with this publication.

- How does the publication offer a distinctive service to fill a market niche?

- Does it employ knowledgeable professionals?

- Who will be working with you? How long have they been employed with this service?

Print Circulation

- Your best indication of coverage is your own experience: do you see the publication in your travels?

- Does the service target advisers, teachers, and agencies, or is it directed to students and their parents, or both?

- Is it intended as a reference or is it a take-home handbook?

- How is the magazine distributed? What is the circulation?

- Does it focus on a specific market segment, i.e. summer, youth, or executive programs? U.S. or Canadian programs?

- How does the publisher obtain, develop, and maintain the mailing list? Does the publisher utilize local representatives in major cities?

- Does the service provide translation and proofreading?

WEB SITE TRAFFIC

- How long has the site been in operation?

- How does the site build traffic?

- How do I track results; what reports do I receive?

- Am I getting unique inquiries? Does the site allow students to send inquiries to more than one school at a time?

- How user-friendly for international students is the site?

- How many unique visitors does the site get (not "hits")? What are the top 20 countries in terms of traffic?

- Is the site multilingual? Can I have my content translated into other languages? Can I post these translations on my own Web site?

Adapted with permission of www.studyUSA.com

How do you turn inquiries into matriculated students? Start by ensuring that you have "multiple points of contact" with prospective students. Also develop a reliable labeling and tracking system for leads. Marketers at a university in Hawaii designed a short, discrete "jump page" URL for ads they ran in two editions of a U.S. recruitment magazine. After a year they were pleased at the results: at least one thousand direct e-mails to their site, not counting repeat visits. You may not be quite as fortunate, especially if your campus is not located in Honolulu; however, the experiment illustrates the effectiveness of print in driving traffic to the Internet and the advisability of installing some sort of system to tabulate that incoming traffic.

Many international admissions offices create and maintain e-mail response templates they can send immediately, depending upon subject matter. Electronic media—CDs, video, e-brochures—can be part of your outreach, again at a lower cost than travel. Some campus Web sites feature streaming videos of international students speaking to visitors. E-mail newsletters can also be useful in recruiting.

Although student search services or purchasing international student names are options, be aware that reliable agencies usually have privacy policies that preclude sharing such contact information. Moreover, lists of names can provide you with quantity but not necessarily quality of applicants.

Print

Print is instrumental to your international outreach, even more so in other countries than in the United States. Students (and parents) appreciate having something tangible to take home. Presenting information on paper truly legitimizes your institution with parents and advisers. Brochures and magazines are easy to read and to share with others.

To advertise, you can choose among many directories designed for international students. Some are general reference guides while others focus on specific levels of study (M.B.A.) or time of year (summer.) They may be country-specific (United States or Canada) and translated into key overseas languages. Advertise in overseas daily newspapers when you are planning to visit major cities. The cost may be high though, so allocate your dollars wisely and keep your message short.

When you travel overseas, you'll see frayed and faded posters still adorning the walls of educational advising agencies. Send or bring them something fresh and up-to-date to display. You will also require brochures when you travel. With Internet-based printers, you now can afford to print in the United States and bring flyers in your luggage although many admission officials prefer to send them ahead via UPS or FedEx or overseas bulk carriers.

Social Media

Web 2.0 technology has spawned the creation of interactive social media such as networking sites, bulletin boards, blogposts, podcasts, wikis and video conferencing. Your prospective students who used to visit Internet cafes now use their mobile phones to check Facebook, watch YouTube, Twitter and text message their friends. Over the next few years, students will clearly favor their mobile phones over their PC's. Be sure your site is built to display on a mobile device. You may want to install foreign language subtitles on your recruiting videos, or better yet, record students in their own languages.

Advertising Do's and Don'ts for International Recruiters	
Do . . .	**Don't . . .**
• Find and stress your program's Find and stress your program's "comparative advantage," what differentiates it from others.	• Use long, complex sentences or idiomatic American slang (i.e., world of opportunity).
• Keep text brief. Use short phrases and simple vocabulary.	• Limit maps to showing a single state, show the entire United States or your region instead.
• Do use professional quality photos, not amateur snapshots. Show both U.S. and international students doing something interesting, i.e. using high-tech equipment, listening or speaking in class, meeting with a professor, holding a test tube, walking across campus, or enjoying a field trip.	• List the number of degrees you award; instead mention majors that are popular with international students.
	• Show pictures containing students of only one ethnic group.
• Motivate students to request information. On your site, use a form to streamline data.	• Use time-dated information. Instead say "Early June to mid-August" rather than "June 5–August 12, 2012.")
• Develop an uncluttered layout, plenty of white space, easy-to-read type. List bullet items rather than complete sentences, especially for ESL programs.	• Use photos of classes on the campus lawn, bare arms and feet, people making V-signs with their fingers, or eating because these can all mean something very different in different cultures.
• Keep Web screens short. Limit scrolling to 1-1/4 screens of text.	• Use toll-free telephone numbers.
• Spell out state names (Colorado, not CO), and include "U.S.A." in your address.	
• Because "college" equals "high school" overseas, use the terms "university-level education" or "university degree" unless there is a name conflict.	
• Invest in accurate translation.	

Adapted with permission of www.studyUSA.com

With so many options for communicating with prospective students, your challenges are to: 1) understand the strengths (and weaknesses) of the various media; 2) incorporate the message conveyed via social media into your overall marketing strategy; and 3) learn what is working and why. A good place to start is with your recently enrolled international students. They'll be pleased to help you stay current with students in their country.

You can also use social networking sites, banner ads, mobile phone messaging, and other online sources to reach potential applicants. To get a sense of how colleges and universities are using these tools, see *Social Media and College Admissions: The First Longitudinal Study* conducted by Nora Ganim Barnes and Eric Mattson at www.umassd.edu/cmr/studiesresearch/mediaandadmissions.pdf. Also see the section Cyber Recruitment Resources in Appendix A.

When to Say It

Generally, print publications for international students appear on school shelves conveniently in time for the decisionmaking season—for the northern hemisphere, in autumn. Understandably, magazines destined for Latin America are published early in the year. If you are promoting a summer program, join a service whose publications are available January to June.

You can coordinate your message with special timetables—for example after national exam results are announced in locations such as Hong Kong and Japan, where there are limited options for "average" students to enter university.

Free Publicity

Your own students are your best recruiters; interview them for ads, brochures, and news articles, ask to take their photos in class and on campus and get written permission to use their photos. Meet them in their home cities after they graduate when you're recruiting there. Prospective students may find current students and recent graduates more credible than your admissions recruiters (see Chapter 4.2: Making the Most of Alumni Contacts).

Your professors, too, can influence prospective students and their parents. When your faculty travel overseas, arm them with brochures and schedule meetings with prospective students and their families.

International recruiting publications are eager for byline articles. Seize this opportunity. Ask the editor what you can contribute. Use the media to describe the advantages of studying abroad, using your institution's strengths as examples.

Send publicity photos to publications where you advertise. Print publications require high-resolution image files. Every time you have a professional photo shoot, send new files to the editor. Your caption or "credit line" under an attractive photo is tantamount to a free advertisement.

If you take the initiative, you will "get what you pay for"…and much more.

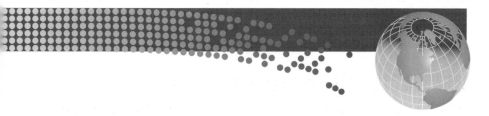

Chapter 3.2

International Travel

Louis Gecenok

Things have progressed since the early days of international student recruitment travel in the 1980s, when it was generally viewed as the be-all and end-all of international student recruitment. Several new phenomena, either not present prior to September 11, 2001 or of too little significance to matter, have now become important and integral to the international student recruitment scene. Perhaps most significant of these is the burgeoning use of the Internet that has irrevocably altered the central focus on travel in international recruitment plans. Millions of potential students abroad now have access to the Internet and are using it to search university Web sites for the information that could lead them to you. With a few keystrokes they can instantly have information that previously took a couple of weeks to arrive by postal mail (at considerable institutional expense) and can easily compare your offerings to those of multiple competitors.

Nevertheless, international travel remains an extremely productive part of the recruitment plan. It may no longer be the only game in town nor the most cost-effective means, but it remains the heart of many recruitment plans because it is the personal contacts with counselors, students, and their families that often close the deal—connections that cannot be made long distance. Mindful of that, recruitment travel should be undertaken only after the institution incorporates it into its *strategic* plan. The institution must be prepared to insure that the added student inquiries generated from international travel will be handled expeditiously to maximize the results of their international efforts. As we will see throughout this chapter, prompt, effective follow-up is essential to success.

Compared to internet recruitment modalities, international travel immediately demonstrates to other countries that an institution is actively investing time, effort, and funds in international education. At the same time, the institution gathers direct knowledge about the political and cultural landscape and people visited. Personal contact with counselors, educational ministry officials, students, and parents enables the university representative to increase his/her understanding of how educational systems in the target countries are organized and function. It also provides an unparalleled opportunity for travelers to experience and understand the world that their students come from and how best to address students' cultural and educational needs on campus. Your decision to travel will depend on a variety of factors.

Who Should Be the Recruiter?

Who is best suited to be the recruiter for your institution? The answer will come from the organizational structures in place at your particular university, and the skills and experience of staff members. Sometimes the responsibility will fall to one individual and sometimes to several, depending on institutional size, the kinds of students sought, and the institution's level of commitment to international educational exchange. Recruiters will most often be part of the admission office, international admission office, international student advising office, or faculty.

Whatever your institutional structure, international travel must never be viewed as a junket or awarded to someone as a perk. Because it is your most central recruitment activity, its success or failure depends upon the positive recognition of your institution abroad and its ability to realize its international education plans. It is incumbent upon institutions to send representatives who have been given enough time and resources to plan adequately for the trip. In addition to good public relations skills, they need cross-cultural sensitivity and interest, an understanding of the educational systems of the United States and the countries to be visited, and knowledge of the full range of academic programs offered by their own institution. They should be prepared to engage in a multitude of varying activities, for long days and evenings, and to follow through on their responsibilities.

Group Tours

A group tour offers particular advantages as an institution's first overseas recruitment trip. Having an experienced tour provider take care of essential logistical planning for the trip is the principal advantage, and one that should not be underestimated. Scheduling two or three weeks of overseas appointments can be extremely challenging. Coordinating flights, hotels, and recruitment visits requires a tremendous expenditure of time, effort, planning, and patience. Schedules have to be created and recreated numerous times as appointments are made, cancelled, or rescheduled. Even the most experienced recruiters may find the amount of time required to organize a trip to be beyond their resources. Those new to international recruitment are cautioned to think carefully before attempting to coordinate a first tour on their own.

Selecting a Tour

Consider these variables when deciding on a particular recruitment tour:

- Length of trip: typically two or more weeks at a time

- Pace: usually two or three days per city, then off to the next, working seven days a week

- Number of participants: typically anywhere from 10 to 50

- Cost: price varies with coverage (education fairs only, or airfare, hotels, some meals, etc.)

- Recruitment focus: undergraduate, graduate, M.B.A.

- Related educational opportunities: briefings, in-country materials

- Record of success and past participants' recommendations

Be especially careful to consider the reputation of the tour organizer. The students and counselors you meet will associate your institution with the tour and the other participating institutions. An inappropriate match may work against your institution's image. When contemplating your first trip, ask colleagues that you know and respect for their evaluations of different tour providers. Currently, numerous group tours operate throughout Asia, Latin America, Europe, India, and the Middle East, with schedules available in the fall or spring. Sub-Saharan Africa, though still a new and comparatively small market, has seen the start-up of group tours as has Eastern Europe and Scandinavia.

There are now recruitment tour groups that focus toward certain student populations such as community college, undergraduate, or graduate students exclusively, or on M.B.A. students, fine arts, or performing arts students. Some may have a state or regional focus. Some include private, boarding high school representatives in the tour, and some allow participation by non-U.S. institutions.

Perhaps the most common purpose of the tour organizer is to stage college fairs for the institutions represented on the tour. The fairs may be held in a hotel ballroom or at a local exhibition center, where they may be open to the general public. Fairs are often held on the campus of a local high school or university, in which case they may be restricted to the students of the school and perhaps a few other participating schools. For detailed information about overseas fairs, see Chapter 3.3: Recruitment Fairs.

Some group tours include an educational component, such as briefings with ministry of education officials of the countries visited, the educational attaché from the U.S. consulate, professors at local universities, bi-national centers, or the staff of organizations such as the Fulbright Commission and AMIDEAST. These briefings can encompass current economic and political events, emerging student market trends, and recent educational developments. They provide an excellent means to improve your understanding of an educational system in the context of that country's culture and history.

Important additional sources of learning on the group tour, often taken for granted, are the experienced institutional representatives with whom you travel. On the plane, in the airport, on buses, and while sharing meals, you will have considerable time to discuss the subtleties of international recruitment, the "do's and don'ts," successes and failures, foreign credential evaluation issues, and other subjects. At its best, an overseas group recruitment tour is not only your most effective recruitment activity, but also a traveling seminar in international education.

Group travel also has its disadvantages. The post-9/11 travel environment has created a maze of airport logistical headaches for groups to negotiate. It's not as easy as it once was to arrange for group baggage check-in, or for the tour leader to present everyone's tickets at the check-in counter. Current travel security measures often require the entire group to arrive at the airport three hours before each flight.

Some recruitment tours still offer a fixed itinerary for all participants. Although this provides benefits of scale that lower the costs associated with transportation and lodging, it can limit the degree to which the program can address the needs of individual schools. Your institution might be interested in the recruitment of undergraduate students only, yet the tour might include some venues designed to attract graduate students. Or your institution may be trying to increase enrollments in its intensive English program, but the tour could focus on the recruitment of American students living abroad, or on students in American or other English-speaking schools. Some groups will allow members to schedule individual appointments at such times, others will insist on full group participation at all scheduled events.

Although most group tour organizers are careful to schedule their trips at the best possible time of the year to reach interested students, the timing may not be ideal for you. It may be inconvenient to be gone for the length of time required, or you may have conflicting plans. Institutions new to overseas recruitment, and as a new member in a group of institutions that may have longstanding relationships, may find gaining recognition and acceptance by overseas counselors or students challenging. Be patient, and always be prepared to step forward and present your institution when the opportunity arises.

Other disadvantages are that your group recruitment tour may also visit countries in which you have little interest or exclude countries you would like to visit. In these situations, a significant portion of your overseas travel time may not be directed at your primary focus so the yield on your investment will likely be diminished. Look for tours that offer you the flexibility to customize your itinerary, to skip or to stay longer in another city or country that has more potential for you.

Individual and Blended Travel

The disadvantages of group recruitment travel, or the lessons one learns during group travel, may lead you to construct an individual trip and itinerary tailored to your institutional interests. Make sure, though, that you have sufficient institutional commitment, support staff, and time available to carry you through the time-consuming, complicated process of planning and scheduling your trip.

The representative traveling alone will have to begin thinking very early in the planning about the countries to be visited and the events and appointments to be made. As a first-time exercise, it is advisable to start at least a full year in advance by constructing a planning calendar. The advantages of establishing your own itinerary are that you can select the countries you want to visit, stay as long as you need, and make appointments that are appropriate for your school. With the assistance of an experienced travel agent, you will be able to find appropriate hotels at corporate or discounted rates and the most efficient airline routes. Select your travel agent carefully, and make sure they understand that you may change your itinerary several times before your planning is completed.

In recent years, more U.S. universities have established institutional linkages with overseas universities, such as faculty or student exchanges, joint degree programs, and research collaborations. Individual travel affords you the opportunity to spend some quality time with your existing institutional partners to renew and enhance programs that have gone dormant, and to build new programs where you already are known and have established a working relationship.

Perhaps the primary advantage of traveling alone is the opportunity to arrange individual appointments where the focus is one-on-one communication about your institution. Appointments can include off-campus visits with students, alumni, consular officials and agents, as well as campus visits with school counselors and students. Such visits, usually held in a less chaotic atmosphere than that of a college fair, allow you to present the unique programs of your institution and to tailor your comments to the students and counselors you are visiting. The experienced recruiter will schedule a variety of appointments to best address the institution's enrollment goals and the demands of their travel schedule.

In many countries, four and five-star hotel lobbies are commonly used for business meetings by hotel guests. Use the lobby as a comfortable, convenient, and cost-free place to have scheduled individual meetings with prospective students and their families over tea or coffee. Meeting in your hotel room is not advisable. Meeting rooms in the hotel can be booked for a dinner event with a group of alumni, or for a presentation to a small gathering of prospective students, allowing the hotel's prestige to be extended to you and to your university.

Organizations such as Fulbright Commissions and the Institute of International Education (IIE) sponsor large international education fairs throughout Europe, Asia, and Latin America each fall. In addition, most tour organizers now offer university representatives the option of participating in their fairs without being a member of the tour. The advantage is that the individual recruiter has multiple opportunities to contact large numbers of prospective students without being tied to a group tour. Because the timing of these fairs is coordinated within the region, they provide a convenient framework for an itinerary that will include individual visits and meetings.

The challenge to the combination of organized fairs and independent travel is two-fold: schools will often be too busy with the group to accommodate your individual visit, and coordinating your individual itinerary to link up with the occasional group fair is even more complicated than a purely individual travel plan. However, for experienced recruiters who have solid travel planning support, know their institutional recruitment goals well, and have accrued knowledge and successful experience representing their institution abroad, a blend of individual and group travel offers the best of both worlds.

Scheduling

Making and rescheduling recruitment trip appointments ahead of time is now quicker, easier, and less expensive because of global e-mail. However, always be sure to confirm your appointments in writing and be explicit concerning the specific arrangements for each visit planned. In your confirmation letter, reiterate the purpose of your visit and the amount of time your schedule allows. Upon arrival in the city, call schools to reconfirm appointments. Get maps and directions in English and the local language. Allow time between visits in case your appointment takes longer than expected, and allow for delays or last minute changes in the format of your meeting.

It is best to approach individual travel with a sense of adventure—expect the unexpected! When changes are needed, as they often are, try to accommodate everyone even if the revised schedule isn't the most convenient for you; your flexibility and graciousness will be remembered. Whatever the type of visit, send a packet with as much appropriate information as possible before you go and carry another packet with you, to present personally in case the one you sent was not received. When deciding what information to send and take, don't assume that the counselors, professors, or agents with whom you will be meeting know anything about U.S. higher education in general, or about your institution in particular. They may not be aware of any of their previous students that have attended your school. They may not know much about the U.S. university application process (or conversely, they may have graduated from a U.S. university!). Try to assess their level of knowledge as much as possible, but be sure to be culturally sensitive and avoid making assumptions.

Needless to say, all of these activities need to be planned well in advance. In particular, be well prepared for first-time visits to schools and universities. Begin by identifying "feeder" schools, schools from which your institution has enrolled good students in the past and others that could become good sources of students. Many, if not most, countries will have American or international schools abroad. They are excellent sources of undergraduate students who have been exposed to a U.S.-pattern curriculum. Typically, the student body will be one-third Americans, one-third local, and one-third third-country nationals. In many countries you will also find highly qualified students at elite national schools. If your focus is to recruit graduate students, target local universities, and arrange meetings where possible at the local Fulbright and other international educational advising offices.

When requesting appointments at host-country schools, keep in mind that the primary concern of the high school counselor or the university faculty member often is to send their students to local universities and graduate programs. They may have little interest in, or may in fact be somewhat opposed to, sending their students to U.S. institutions. Part of your responsibility as an international educator will be to explain the benefits for their students and promote goodwill on behalf of U.S. higher education in general. Don't write off such counselors or faculty members because they could develop into good recruitment sources. Consider making regular courtesy visits over the years in hopes of helping them broaden their views of your institution and of U.S. higher education.

Costs

It often comes as a surprise that the cost of individual travel differs from that of group travel, not necessarily the total amount spent but in how it is spent. If you opt for individual travel, you and your institution will decide how much money to allocate on venues for large group events. You will decide whether or not you can afford individual advertising, brochures, or announcements in local media—knowing that it will cost much more than when shared by a large group. Remember, though, that any individual advertising you purchase will be specific to your institution and may be worth the additional costs involved. If you elect not to produce a special brochure to use on the trip, as most participants in group tours do, the money saved can be put toward other uses such as other advertising; a reception for prospective students and their parents, for parents of currently enrolled students, or for an alumni gathering; or for visiting additional countries.

Mailing brochures to use during an individual university recruitment visit is costly. Plan ahead and take advantage of international remailers or bulk surface mail rates for any large event. Use military post office (APO and FPO) addresses if available for any large sponsored events because they require domestic rather than international postage—but delivery time is considerably longer. You could ultimately pay more for these items than if traveling with a group that arranges a group rate for shipping your materials. Make sure that you include a way to track and find materials that may become delayed or lost, and do allow plenty of delivery time in case there is a delay.

Follow-Up

A well-planned and executed recruitment trip overseas requires the same planning and execution in the follow-up with prospective students and with the alumni, counselors, and advisers you met during your travels. See After the Fair in Chapter 3.3: Recruitment Fairs for excellent suggestions on how to follow-up with students. Correspondence with alumni should be coordinated with the alumni office (see Chapter 4.2: Making the Most of Alumni Contacts). Finally, while the prospective students are the primary focus of your travel, it is the relationships you develop with the overseas advisers and school counselors that will continue to pay off in the years to come. Happy travels!

Advantages and Disadvantages of Group Recruitment Travel

Advantages

- Multiple schools attract larger crowds. You will meet more prospective students.

- It expands your network of professional colleagues. You will learn from them while traveling.

- Most tour organizers provide you with orientation to the countries and their educational systems to help you when meeting with students.

- All arrangements are included in the fee, making it efficient and cost effective for you.

- The cost of events, advertising, and transportation is shared. One school cannot afford to do for itself what a group can do together.

- Local personnel being visited often prefer to serve many schools with one effort.

Disadvantages

- There is seldom enough time for you to explain your programs to the local personnel being visited.

- Your school may not stand out among the schools of the tour.

- The itinerary may include places or programs that are not useful for your institution.

- The timing of the tour may not fit your schedule.

- There may be schools or individuals in the group with whom you do not want to be associated.

Advantages and Disadvantages of Individual and Blended Recruitment Travel

Advantages

- The itinerary can be adjusted to meet the needs of your institution.

- Your recruitment can be tailored and directed to a specific audience.

- All of the appointments will be relevant to your institution.

- Time can be scheduled to explore the environment and identify new opportunities for your institution.

- When you make a visit, local personnel connect you to your institution.

- Meeting personally with school and agency officials gives you the opportunity to explain your programs and the distinguishing characteristics of your school.

- There may be time and opportunity for longer, more in-depth meetings and/or interviews with prospective students and their parents.

- Through visits and meetings, you have the opportunity to learn about the students in their educational and cultural context, and be better able to make good decisions about their ability to perform at your institution.

Disadvantages

- You will see fewer students.

- Advertising in multiple countries is costly.

- It is time consuming to make all the arrangements for an individual tour.

- It is more expensive to do presentations to groups of students.

- You do not get any feedback or information from travel companions.

- Individual travel can be lonely.

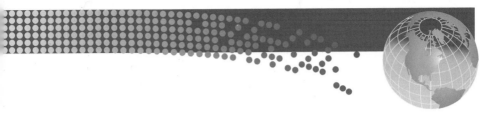

Recruitment Fairs

Marjorie S. Smith

• • • •

Electronic recruitment solutions, Web-based inquiry management, online application systems and brand consultancy are now commonplace amongst International and Student Recruitment Offices. But as a means of facilitating the relationship between prospective students and institutions, modern technology has yet to surpass the education fair as one of the primary vehicles for successful student recruitment.

—*Tim Rogers*
London School of Economics and Political Science,
IIE Network Newsletter, 2007

Overseas recruitment fairs have been around as long as colleges and universities have been traveling together to recruit international students. They can take place in a hotel ballroom, a school auditorium, a cafeteria, exhibition hall, or stadium. They can attract thousands of students or only a few. In the best case, a well-advertised and well-attended fair will put your school's name in the minds of many who may not otherwise be familiar with your programs. It can be a means to build your prospect pool, to affect focused follow-up, and it can be a chance to speak with students' parents, whose influence is essential to the college selection process. It can also be an opportunity to make individual appointments with 'hot prospects' later in your visit.

Recruitment fairs are not a magic bullet, however. No successful recruitment plan is based solely on fair participation. Remember, some can be poorly attended or attract students different from those you seek. Some can be so crowded that you never have a chance to make an impression; you are simply handing out brochures and answering basic questions. Be prepared for all of these scenarios and determine how you can maximize the experience for your school and the students.

Finding the Best Fair for Your Institution

When comparing fairs, here are some questions to ask:

- What is the history of a given fair? What are the attendance statistics for the last few years? How many undergraduate versus graduate prospects? In what fields?

- Who runs or manages it? There are some fair organizers who do nothing but plan and execute recruitment fairs. There are others whose main business may be something else entirely. This can be a quality clue. Regardless, getting references is a necessity.

- What are the costs to schools? Exhibitors can be charged anything from $400 for a three-hour fair and a table in a school gymnasium to $4000 for a two-day fair and a booth in an exhibition hall. It is important to investigate what the costs include and exclude.

- Is there a cost to students? Many reputable education fairs have no cost for students to attend. Others will charge only enough to discourage casual pen-collectors and the mildly curious. Still others will charge hefty amounts from students and institutions alike. If you intend to invite your current inquiry pool to the fair, be sure to let them know if there is an entrance fee.

- Does the timing fit other calendar events? Recruitment fairs were once only an autumn or spring phenomenon, but they now happen all over the world in every season. It is much easier to plan travel during times that are most advantageous to the institution (avoiding the heavy "reading season" or student orientations and graduations.) Another timing consideration is the education calendar in the country or city you are visiting. One strategy would be to choose fairs that occur after national examination results are released. Students, parents, and college representatives will all have a better idea of a student's admissibility or eligibility for scholarships. Likewise, any reputable fair organizer will avoid conflicting with important examinations or religious holidays.

- Is it part of a circuit? A "circuit" is where fairs are organized in a planned sequence in different cities or countries in a region. Recruiters are expected to make their own travel and hotel arrangements. Likewise, recruiters may choose as many or as few fairs as they wish. The advantages of participating in more than one fair while you are in the area are that it is cost-effective and convenient—but circuit travel is also safer and less lonely. A few examples of circuit travel are the Institute of International Education fairs in Asia and the Mexico College Fair Tour organized by international high school counselors there. Additionally, some recruitment tours offer a "fairs only" option to schools interested in customizing their recruitment trips or looking for ways to stretch their recruitment budgets.

- Who attends? Is the fair targeted to a certain segment of students or is it open to any and all? Will you be spending more of your time saying "we don't have that program" or talking about how your programs are distinctive?

- How is the fair advertised to students? Good advertising is key to a successful fair. Ask the organizers where they advertise, how often, and when.

- Are registration lists provided? Some fair organizers provide the names and contact information for all students attending the fairs. This information, if it includes the students' intended level of study and major, can be used to contact students that fit your profile. You should confirm that these lists are not shared with or sold to institutions that did not attend the fair.

- Who may participate or exhibit? We are often judged by "the company we keep," so be sure you are comfortable with the exhibitor criteria. Are recruiting agents invited to have booths? Are trade schools? Is the fair limited to schools from the United States? Must all schools be accredited? Are there NAFSA or National Association of College Admission Counseling (NACAC) members? Are there enough schools like your own or too many? Fair organizers should be able to provide you with their selection criteria and a list of exhibitors who attended their most recent fair.

- Who may represent the institution? Another quality clue is to determine the criteria for the school representatives. Some require campus-based employees. Some require a certain amount of recruitment experience. Some have no criteria at all. Many will limit the number of representatives at each table (usually two or three). Ask whether alumni may join you behind the table.

- Is there a public service component? Some fair organizers invite local EducationUSA officers to speak to the attendees about their services. State Department officials responsible for issuing visas can answer questions about the visa application process. Institutions may present an overview of U.S. higher education to the audience, along with information about scholarships, application requirements, and strategies for presenting a winning application. Fairs with a public service component are both helpful to the audience and will attract more students hoping to learn the basics.

- How long are the fairs? It's important to be present when the fair is in process, so be sure to commit to the days, dates, and specific hours. When are the breaks?

- Will translators be available? Some fairs will offer a host or "translator" to help you communicate with students and (especially) parents.

How do you learn about fairs? Aside from the mailings and e-mail messages you will receive from fair organizers, these two Web sites keep a comprehensive and up-to-date list of overseas recruitment fairs, by country, date, and links to the organizers.

1. U.S. Journal.com (www.usjournal.com/en/students/info/fairs.html)

2. EducationUSA.state.gov (www.educationusa.state.gov/fairs.htm)

These are particularly useful when you have a region or a particular time of year in mind and want to know what fairs are available within your school's desired parameters.

Planning for a Fair

Be sure you are sending the right person. Recruitment fairs require a great deal of stamina—some can be overcrowded, hot, and/or very long. Students and parents may speak in low voices and/or with minimal English skills, requiring a lot of patience and courtesy by your representative. They should have an easy smile and a welcoming manner. Whoever stands behind the table must be able to talk intelligently about all programs at your school. Whether you send the dean or the ESL director, they must be prepared.

Before Going

- Invite your current prospects and applicants.

- Invite any alumni living near the fair location.

- Invite the parents of your current students.

What to Bring

- Something for everyone—Have enough of something with your school's logo and/or Web site (a brochure, bookmark, or business card) to give to everyone. The fair organizers should have detailed information recommending the amount of material you should have, as well as shipping information.

- College tablecloth for your exhibit space.

- Detailed list of departments and contacts—While you must know the minimum details about all your programs, you cannot know everything. Have a list of all departments, majors, and contacts to give to students who have specific curricular questions.

- Inquiry cards—Even if there is a registration system, some students are just more comfortable filling out a card. And if there isn't such a system, these cards become the backbone to measure the effectiveness of the fair.

- Display—Stand-up displays are eye-catching and helpful in answering basic questions (programs, cost, test requirements, scholarships, maps, and pictures) allowing more time for deeper conversations.

- Business cards.

What to Wear

- Business suit (It is the most appropriate for indoor and evening fairs.)

- School polo shirt and khakis (These are the most appropriate for outdoor fairs and secondary school visits.)

- Name tag

- Comfortable shoes

- When in doubt, dress conservatively.

While You Are There

How should you talk to students? Because many students will have already researched your school on the Internet, make the fair productive and different from an online experience. Find out more about the students so that you can make a personal connection between their needs and interests, and your programs and offerings.

Most students have two big questions they want answered: Can I get in? Can I afford it? Both are difficult questions for them to ask, so don't wait for them. Go ahead and tell students what your requirements are, how much it costs to go there, scholarship availability, and the admission criteria. Provided you still have their attention, begin explaining the value of the educational experience at your school.

If students aren't admissible or can't afford to attend, you have an opportunity to set proper expectations. Give students an alternative (suggest another school, refer them to EducationUSA officers, or suggest community college alternatives). Also, it is a common complaint among students who attend fairs that representatives don't know about their program of interest ("Sorry, I'm here representing the undergraduate programs. Here's the Web site you can visit for more information about XYZ.") Make it your goal to have every student walk away from your table happy and informed...even those who will never enroll.

Recruitment Fair Behavior

Different fairs have different rules, but the most professional ones will enforce a uniform, equal playing field, free from gimmicks and the "hard sell." The following commonly accepted no-no's will be standard at most U.S. recruitment fairs overseas:

- Giveaways—Students should be drawn to your table for information, not giveaways. Pens, bookmarks, and DVDs are standard items that schools will give out to students, along with brochures. However, tee-shirts, raffles, key chains, or any other gimmicks to get students to come to your table are usually not allowed. Plus, it cheapens the experience—fairs can turn into a "gotta get the cool mousepad from North America Community College" rather than "I've got to sit with this fair guide and figure out the best match for my academic goals." So, if no schools bring these things, everyone has a fair shake.

- Standing in front of your table—Standing in front of your table or booth may give you the appearance of being more approachable, but it also creates what some might say is too casual an atmosphere. It invites more individual conversations, making it difficult for other passersby to hear or learn. Keeping a formal distance between you and the student allows for a public conversation, invites others to approach and look at the table display while you finish your conversation, and creates a more inviting situation for everyone. Related to this, alumni and local representatives sometimes roam the room directing students to their school's table. This too is usually not permissible at recruitment fairs.

- Leaving early—It can be very tempting to pack up when there are only a few people in the room. However, when advertisements and your own communication have stated you will be there until a certain time, you must be there. Nothing will irritate your prospects more than making the effort to see you at a fair, only to find that you have already left. When things like this happen, you do far more damage to your recruitment effort than if you never attended the fair at all.

NACAC's National College Fair Exhibitor Guidelines are considered the gold standard for recruitment fair practices, www.nacacnet.org/EventsTraining/CollegeFairs/Exhibitor/Pages/default.aspx.

Other Tips

- Get your rest. Eat a meal. Take a break before you get cranky (leave nothing valuable at your table).

- Don't shout. It's cliché, but true: representatives will sometimes speak very loudly, especially in crowded situations and when speaking to those with weak English skills.

- Don't take anything of value to the fair. Keep your money/ID/hotel key close to you.

- Learn to manage a crowd of students. Some fairs can be so crowded that you find yourself answering a question, only to have the next person (who wedged their way in) ask the same question—or interrupt to get their question answered. One effective method is to tell the students gathered around that you will answer questions in a clockwise fashion. When you finish answering questions from left to right, you will then start at the beginning. Advise students to listen carefully to the questions asked since they may hear the information they seek.

- What do you do if the fair is poorly attended? Turn lemons into lemonade! At the other end of the spectrum, despite the efforts of the organizers and advertising, some fairs are simply not well attended. When this happens, take advantage of the opportunity to have longer and better conversations with students and parents. When you aren't talking to a student, remain attentive and approachable. Consider walking away from the table for a short time—students tend to gravitate to unattended tables perhaps because it is less intimidating. If this happens and they seem to linger, go over and introduce yourself.

After the Fair

It is essential that you have a communication plan set up for staying in touch with the students you've met. Here is a sample plan to consider:

- You will probably meet a handful of particularly strong candidates at each fair. E-mail those students as soon as possible after the fair. Remind them of your conversation (use a tag phrase or mention a defining program that will spark their memory).

- If you promised to follow up with information or certain contacts, do this as soon as possible.

- Send postcards or handwritten notes to the same strong candidates while you are still travelling.

- Send these same students' contact information to key colleagues on campus asking them to follow up with mailings, messages, or even phone calls.

- When you get back to campus, get the cards or registration lists loaded into your database as soon as possible. Be sure you have a way to code the records so that you can track them back to a particular fair.

- Send a personalized, mail-merged e-mail message to every student as soon as possible. Highlight the same distinctive features that you talked about in your fair presentation.

- Send something by snail mail. Students are rarely reading e-mail with their parents, but they may open their mail and share a brochure or letter. Paper communication is particularly important when it comes to parents.

- Consider including an "action item" in your communications, requiring students to contact you for something (brochure on writing an effective essay, tips on what colleges look for etc.) or an incentive for applying (e.g., application fees will be waived for students applying by a certain date, priority scholarship consideration, and so on).

- Set up a regular communication plan that will exclude students who don't respond and pursue those that do. Subsequent communication can include letters from alumni, current students, and club representatives.

Return on Your Investment

In this age of Internet communication, Web sites and electronic advertising, the recruitment fair remains a powerful tool for introducing our schools to a selected segment of the overseas student population. By visiting those countries and participating in those fairs specifically targeting the kinds of students we want to attract, we can affect a more direct return on our recruitment dollar. With proper planning, execution and follow-up, recruitment fairs can be an excellent investment.

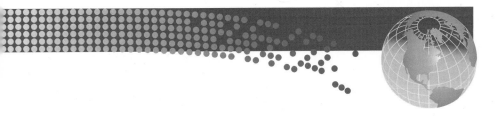

Working with Sponsored Students

Rebecca Smith-Murdock, Aleka Myre, and Tracy Kaan

The decision to recruit sponsored students puts an institution or program on yet another roller coaster ride in the ever-changing world of international education. It is a rewarding and exhilarating experience, but there are ups and downs, twists and turns. Over the past three decades, U.S. international educators have seen both sudden ascents and precipitous declines in numbers for many sponsored student groups. English language programs, colleges, and universities have welcomed the arrival and lamented the departure of sponsored students from countries around the world, sponsored by a variety of funding sources with a variety of motivations and goals: Malaysia, Venezuela, Saudi Arabia, Oman, Yeman, and United Arab Emirates, funded by large home government programs; Harari-funded Lebanese; Latin Americans involved in the Kissinger initiatives; Thai students and scholars on a large variety of scholarship programs; Clinton Scholars from the Palestinian Authority; Saudis, again, with a 129 percent increase in the numbers of students in the United States between 2005-06 and 2006-07;[1] Chinese, Kazakhs, Libyans, Chileans, and most recently Iraqis, among many others.

In addition to the typically temporary flows of relatively large numbers of sponsored students, there have also been small, steady, less mercurial sources of students such as the Fulbright program through the Institute of International Education (IIE), the Latin American Scholarship Program for American Universities (LASPAU), and AMIDEAST, the Muskie and Humphrey Fellows, and other U.S.-funded initiatives.

Sponsored Student Trends

Although the attention and publicity given to whatever is the most recent large sponsoring project would lead one to believe otherwise, IIE statistics regarding primary sources of funding indicate that a very small percentage of international students in the U.S. are "sponsored" as the term is currently defined. To be sponsored, in the current definition, a student's primary funding for education cannot come from personal resources, the resources of family and friends in any country, or the receiving U.S. college or university. Instead, to be categorized as a sponsored student, primary sources of funding would likely be the student's home government, a home country university, a future or current employer, or an organization or foundation in the student's home country. Other funding sources for a sponsored student could include branches of the U.S. government, U.S. contractors or sub-contractors, or international organizations, foundations, or consortia, among others.

IIE data for the past twenty years (1987-88 through 2006-07) shows a relentless decline in both the absolute number of sponsored students coming to U.S. institutions and in the percentage of international students in the U.S. who are sponsored.[2]

Sponsored International Students in the United States, 1987-2007		
PRIMARY SOURCE OF FUNDS	1987/88	2006/07
Home Government/University	30,720	18,704
U.S. Private Sponsor	9,840	8,003
Foreign Private Sponsor	8,620	6,682
U.S. Government	7,570	3,450
International Organization	2,640	1,685
Total # Sponsored Students	59,390	38,524
Total # International Students	356,190	582,984
% Sponsored Students	16.67	6.61

The visual representation of sponsored student numbers between 1987 and 2007 resembles the downward route of a roller coaster, with ups and downs, but an overall decline. According to the Organisation of Economic Co-Operation and Development, the U.S. total share of international student enrollment fell from 26 percent in 2000 to 22 percent in 2005.[3] IIE data indicates that the U.S. total market share remained at 22 percent in 2006-07. In contrast, during the first half of this decade, the total number of international students in Britain more than doubled.[4] Similarly, Australia, Japan, Germany, and France, among others, have had sharp increases in the numbers of international students.[5]

Certainly, U.S. international educators can recite the litany of causes of this dramatic change: U.S. educational institutions face long-term, well-organized, well-funded, and well-executed competition from Europe, Asia, and Australia. These competitors with the U.S. for both sponsored and nonsponsored students have nationally coordinated marketing plans. In contrast, U.S. institutions generally manage recruitment and marketing at the institutional level, with an occasional regional or state consortium. A recent and telling example of the problems with the U.S. noncentralized approach to recruiting sponsored students has been seen in Iraq. For several years, until August 2008, there was no place in Iraq where the fully sponsored students that the government wanted to send to the U.S. could obtain a student visa. They had to travel to Jordan, Syria, or other countries and wait several months for an interview— using up precious time and money. Even with the announcement of a Baghdad location for visa requests, the U.S. government warned of months-long delays. In contrast, Iraqi Ministry of Education officials have stated that both Britain and Australia have "done a better job than the United States in forging connections with Iraqi universities and helping Iraqi students. A consortium of 24 British universities, working with the British Council, has set up an office in Baghdad to foster links with Iraqi universities, and those recipients of the government scholarships who have applied to British universities have sometimes had their applications processed in a matter of days."[6]

Strong Support Required for Success

While acknowledging the facts of the relatively temporal nature of many sponsoring programs and the statistically small and decreasing number of sponsored students who are coming to the U.S., it is still certainly true that the presence of sponsored students is positive for an educational institution. In addition to contributing to the diversity and internationalization of a program or campus, sponsored students connect a U.S. institution with foreign governments, ministries, universities, agencies, and decisionmakers, which may open other doors for additional special projects and innovative programs initiated either by the U.S. or foreign partner. Furthermore, the presence of sponsored students who are receiving appropriate support services, whose sponsor payments are being received and processed in a timely and organized manner, and who are successfully engaged in a variety of academic programs indicates that there has been a high level of integration of these students' special needs into the school's infrastructure and business practices. The presence of this infrastructure indicates that the U.S. institution has analyzed and dealt with the many procedural, financial, logistical, and intercultural issues that must be managed when sponsored students are thriving on a campus.

An analysis of the financial support/guarantee documents of all the international students at even an institution with weak infrastructural support for sponsored students may indicate that sponsored students have found their way to the campus on their own and are somehow surviving independently. However, to achieve success over time in a deliberate attempt to recruit sponsored students to one's campus will require preliminary analysis, planning, and infrastructure building, and a commitment to long-term internal and external relationship building with sponsoring agencies. And, there is often a need to allow the sponsoring agency to 'certify" that the scores and documents in the application packet are true copies of originals.

Analysis, Planning, and Infrastructure Building

Building a solid, internal infrastructure that will ensure that sponsored students' special needs are met must precede the recruitment of sponsored students. If students arrive and encounter avoidable problems, the institution will lose credibility. Recovering from a bad situation and regaining lost credibility is more difficult work than setting up appropriate systems beforehand. An institution must be willing to ask many questions across a wide range of campus units, probably eliciting complex responses. There are many internal infrastructure systems, processes, and policies that an institution needs to analyze and implement.

Accounting Systems

Not surprisingly, NAFSA's practice resource guide, Monitoring Sponsored Students and Non-Degree Program Participants, asserts that "many sponsored student problems center around funding issues,"[7] so this institutional system and its processes must be examined first.

Is the institution's student accounting unit (e.g., bursar, student accounting office) able to handle third-party billing, invoicing, and delayed payments for sponsored students? Ordinarily, students register and pay their tuition and fees by established deadlines to protect their class registration. In contrast, sponsored students register and then the institution must invoice the sponsor for the students' charges, meanwhile protecting the students' class registration from being voided for nonpayment. For a variety of good and bad reasons, sponsors may not pay promptly. What are the institution's policies and procedures regarding late payments? Are current practices likely to alienate or offend U.S.-based representatives of the sponsoring agencies who are desperately trying to make payments but are unavoidably delayed?

Does the institution already have a modifiable system in place for similar situations, such as the payment of students' tuition by domestic sponsors such as businesses and companies? If it does not, how can the accounting office be persuaded that the benefits of the presence of sponsored students on campus compensate for the work, sometimes quite extensive, that they must undertake to set up a delayed, third-party billing system?

Also, an institution contemplating recruiting sponsored students must analyze whether its accounting or payroll units are set up to allow the institution to receive and distribute students' living allowances without complicating the student's U.S. income tax situation.

All of these first, crucial questions must be asked to units outside the obvious realm of "international education." These units will have their own priorities, and convincing them to allocate personnel, time, and attention to set up systems that will enable the institution to manage sponsored students may be a challenge. However, these questions must be asked and appropriate processes implemented, or a sponsored student recruitment effort cannot succeed.

Tracking, Management, and Reporting Systems

Continuing its internal analysis, an institution preparing to recruit sponsored students must ask which office or offices will assume responsibility for sponsored student tracking, management, and reporting systems. This responsibility includes receiving sponsored students' applications, managing or tracking their progress through the admission system, sending the I-20 or DS2019 forms, maintaining complete files and records on the sponsored students, and communicating systematically, frequently, and helpfully with the student and the sponsor. This person/office must achieve understanding of and adherence to the quite different programmatic requirements and provisions that different sponsors set (e.g., length of scholarship, required visa type, minimum GPA that must be maintained, mandatory summer enrollment, whether working on campus is possible, whether family members may accompany the sponsored students, where the responsibility for medical insurance lies, among many other specific details). The person/office also must fulfill the reporting requirements set by the different sponsors. To assist all offices in the handling of sponsored students, the institution must determine if its computer system is able to identify sponsored students in such a way that everyone who sees the students' records will identify the students as "sponsored," which can eliminate many potential problems.

An institution must determine if it has systems in place that facilitate the inevitable creation of new forms and processes that will result from working with sponsoring agencies. Is there already a release/waiver form so the institutional liaison to the sponsoring agency can access students' records? Is there an insurance-waiver process in case the sponsor provides insurance and the student does not need to purchase the institution's policy? Does the institution's legal office need to be involved in the creation of new forms and processes? If so, how much lead time is required to accomplish the creation of something new through the legal office?

Is the institution prepared to handle potentially complex issues that may appear logical and positive from the standpoint of the student and the education institution but that may be problematic or even prohibited by the sponsoring agency's regulations? These issues might include students' requests to extend funding, to change status from student to postdoctoral researcher, to accept a department's offer of an assistantship, to seek Optional Practical Training, and so on.

Nonacademic Student Services

There is general consensus that good word-of-mouth among sponsored students and sponsoring agencies will increase the numbers of students who are formally or informally referred to an institution. The consistency and quality of nonacademic and academic assistance provided by the institution are key factors in creating good word-of-mouth.

Thus, institutions seeking to recruit sponsored students must assess their ability to provide the extraordinary nonacademic services that may be required by sponsoring agencies. Among the many possibilities are transportation to and from the airport for students' arrivals and departures; guaranteed campus-based housing for undergraduates; assistance with arrangements for apartment leases/utilities/furniture for off-campus housing; specialized and sometimes extensive orientation sessions; free fax and phone access to sponsors by students; immediate assistance when students need medical treatment or counseling; and help with daycare, public school enrollment, and other arrangements when family members accompany the sponsored student. These services will be in addition to the institution's regular assistance to international students with obtaining driver's licenses and/or state identification cards, Social Security cards, bank accounts, and general campus orientation. Institutions may also want or need to consider specialized community programming for sponsored student groups. For example, the University of North Texas arranges to take sponsored student groups to a rodeo, to on-campus football and basketball games, to NASA in Houston, to the Riverwalk in San Antonio, and to concerts on and off campus; other institutions with successful sponsored students programs also provide comparable free or low-cost social, cultural, and educational activities at the request of sponsors or on an on-going basis.

Academic Student Support Services

Academic services to sponsors and sponsored students include acting as a liaison to academic advisers in all the students' departments, sometimes communicating crucial information about unique sponsor requirements and sometimes advocating for students. Ideally, these relationships with decisionmakers within academic departments and the graduate school are seen as long-term, mutually beneficial partnerships. Although crucial, this can be time-consuming. Institutions seeking to recruit sponsored students must spend the necessary time to have support in deed, as well as in word, from academic units that will be particularly attractive to sponsoring agencies.

For colleges and universities, flexibility—without compromising academic standards—will be attractive to sponsored students and sponsoring agencies. This flexibility can be achieved in several ways. For example, the on-campus presence of an effective English as a Second Language program is important for sponsoring agencies that allow students to come to the U.S. before language proficiency requirements are met. It is attractive to students and sponsors if completion of the English language program substitutes for a standardized test score such as TOEFL or IELTS, and it is even more attractive if students in advanced levels of the English language program can combine some regular academic classroom work with their language studies. Another example of helpful flexibility arises from the fact that many sponsored students must have at least conditional or provisional admission in order to receive funding from their sponsor; institutions seeking to enroll sponsored students must assess their institution's willingness and ability to offer conditional or provisional admission to undergraduate and/or graduate students.

Institutions serious about recruiting sponsored students may need to investigate the requirement that scores from U.S-based standardized tests must come with students' application packets. In some countries, access to standardized tests is problematic. The cost, the limited number of testing sites, and students' unfamiliarity with computer-based or Internet-based standardized tests present daunting obstacles. As an example of the effectiveness of flexibility regarding standardized test score requirements, the University of Arkansas at Little Rock, which had 18 Iraqi graduate students in the Spring 2008 semester, "waived the customary Graduate Record Exam and Test of English as a Foreign Language as requirements for Iraqi students. Instead of requiring minimum scores on the tests…the university evaluated[ed] Iraqi students on the basis of their grade-point averages."[6] Furthermore, in many countries, students are given ONE original set of transcripts and other documents for a lifetime; other originals are almost impossible to obtain. Flexibility in accepting copies of such documents, certified by the sponsor or another reliable agency as true copies, will increase a school's ability to recruit sponsored as well as other students from these countries.

Building Relationships with Sponsoring Agencies

The analysis and planning that lead to intra-institutional willingness, flexibility, and capacity will determine the eventual success of external recruitment activity. Intra-institutional relationship building leads to development of the complex infrastructure required to support a successful sponsored student program.

Governments, universities, businesses, and organizations that commit vast amounts of money to support students' academic programs are seeking the highest statistical probability of a positive return on their investment. They want their sponsored students to complete their specifically approved or assigned programs of study in the specified amount of time, and with the fewest impediments. During the student's period of study, the sponsoring agency wants to receive the specified types of reports, in exactly the correct format, and at the specified time. Sponsors want billing processes that meet their particular agency's requirements and that are transparent and comprehensible. When a sponsoring agency can identify educational institutions that consistently fulfill these expectations, making success more likely for their sponsored students, those institutions will remain on the short list for sponsored student referrals or placements.

An institution may be able to have an initial placement of students from a scholarship program simply because of the vastness of the program—such as the Saudi Arabian program that began in 2005. However, to remain on the short list requires delivery on all promises. It also requires the proverbial "relationship building, relationship building, and more relationship building." Positive relationships are based on trust, which comes from trustworthiness. Many actions by institutions demonstrate this trustworthiness: For example, application packets are systematically tracked, and sponsors and students receive frequent, complete communication of both good news and bad news regarding admissibility. Invoices are clear, complete, correct, and transparent. There is up-front explanation of extra charges that will be made to sponsors for the provision of extraordinary services to their sponsored students; ideally, the information will be available on the institution's Web site and in written format. The sponsoring agency is provided with immediate, complete, objective, and helpful information when problems arise. For example, students' difficulties with courses, medical problems, or run-ins with the police are reported quickly and fully and dealt with by the institution helpfully and appropriately.

For their academic-funding programs to work, sponsors want and need effective, judiciously flexible, reliable, and completely honest on-campus partners. The success of any sponsorship program results from well-selected students, well-thought-out policies on the part of the sponsoring agency, and—of equal importance—effective relationships with trustworthy U.S. academic institutions that receive and assist the students.

Clearly, "working with sponsored students" comes at the end of a complex, multidimensional recruitment plan. It comes at the end of an institution's internal processes of analysis, planning, and infrastructure building and its external processes of relationship building with sponsoring agencies. Recruiting a constituency of sponsored students with whom to work is worthwhile on many levels—as a stimulus to infrastructure and relationship building institutionally and as a way to move towards institutional diversity, internationalization, and connectivity with current international education trends.

But hold on—the roller coaster ride is just beginning.

Endnotes

[1] Bhandari, R. & Chow, P. (2007). *Open Doors 2007: Report on International Educational Exchange.* New York, NY: Institute of International Education.

[2] Combined data from *Open Doors: 1948-2004 CD-ROM Report on International Educational Exchange,* http://opendoors.iienetwork.org/?p = 28644, and online at http://opendoors.iienetwork.org/?p = 113123.

[3] Organisation for Economic Co-Operation and Development (OECD). 2007. *Education at a Glance, 2007.* Paris, France: OECD, online at www.oecd.org/edu/eag2007.

[4] Labi, A. 2006. "Foreign Students Increase in Britain." *The Chronicle of Higher Education,* September 22 (53)5, A44.

[5] Council of Graduate Schools. 2008. *Findings from the 2008 CGS International Graduate Admissions Survey.* Accessed June 20, 2008, www.cgsnet.org/portals/0/pdf/R_IntlApps08_I.pdf.

[6] Labi, A. 2008. "Visa Process Keeps Iraqi Students Out of the U.S." *The Chronicle of Higher Education,* (54)27, A1.

[7] NAFSA: Association of International Educators. 1998. *Monitoring Sponsored Students and Non-Degree Program Participants.* Accessed June 13, 2008, from www.nafsa.org/knowledge_community_network.sec/recruitment_admissions/sponsored_program_administration/practice_resources_4/monitoriing/sponsor.

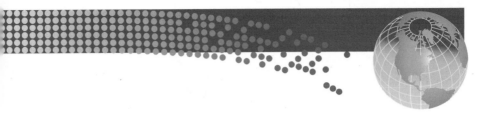

Measuring Results

Cheryl Darrup-Boychuck

In the late 1800s, the famous department store merchant John Wanamaker quipped, "Half the money I spend on advertising is wasted; the trouble is, I don't know which half."

We've come a long way thanks to the power of online marketing and technological advancements in collecting, storing, accessing, and distributing data. Innovative research methods (such as regression analysis and randomization) have also advanced the notion of quantifying reams of qualitative and largely anecdotal information.

That's good news for international admissions counselors, particularly as the older, more experienced counselors begin to retire—and take much of their decades' worth of (largely undocumented) wisdom with them. There's very little hard, historical, economic data in international student admissions. For better or for worse, that's changing. In the 1990s, titles such as "deans of admissions" transformed into "vice presidents of enrollment management." And those corporate-type vice presidents increasingly demand solid justification for every penny in their staff budgets.

Complexity Science

International student recruitment has not and will not evolve into a perfect science because it's practically impossible to define the financial impact of international students. Students seek and discover information about your institution from multiple sources, so it's not very practical to try to determine **exact** cause and effect. For example, some online content, via social networking sites, simply cannot be controlled by official campus representatives; the notion of measuring its effectiveness is even more remote. So it's important to try to reach students via many channels and assess the results with an open mind.

However, accountability is paramount; international student recruiters must develop a solid sense of what's working, and what's not. Fortunately, we now have more sophisticated tools than ever to construct and dissect global promotional campaigns. The process of measuring results in this dynamic field may fall under the auspices of "complexity science," an evolving way of thinking about the world that extends far beyond traditional economic and mathematical models.

As the November 2007 issue of *Harvard Business Review* noted, "Advances in complexity science, combined with knowledge from the cognitive sciences... are poised to help current and future leaders make sense of advanced technology, globalization, intricate markets, cultural change, and much more. In short, the science of complexity can help all of us address the challenges and opportunities we face in a new epoch of human history."

A complex system has the following characteristics (and how they apply to international student recruitment):

- It involves large numbers of interacting elements (millions of prospective international students, along with parents, school counselors, campus-based recruiters, agents paid on commission, faculty, alumni).

- The interactions are nonlinear, and minor changes can produce disproportionately major consequences (well-funded, government-sponsored scholarships from one particular country).

- The system is dynamic, the whole is greater than the sum of its parts, and solutions can't be imposed; rather, they arise from the circumstances. This is frequently referred to as "emergence" (competition among many countries for the best and brightest students in the world).

- The system has a history, and the past is integrated with the present; the elements evolve with one another and with the environment; and evolution is irreversible (global student mobility trends, published by organizations such as the Institute of International Education).

- Though a complex system may, in retrospect, appear to be ordered and predictable, hindsight does not lead to foresight because the external conditions and systems constantly change.

- Unlike ordered systems, where the system (global capacity to place students and scholars) constrains the agents (the students), or chaotic systems, where there are no constraints, in a complex system the agents and the system constrain one another, especially over time. This means that we cannot forecast or predict what will happen.[1]

As the field of complexity science evolves, a sophisticated formula for measuring results in international student recruitment may very well emerge, complete with squiggly lines, Greek characters, and plenty of variables for which colleagues may assign values based on their individual campus circumstances. The challenge is to take into account myriad "quantifiably elusive factors" with varying weights. For example, are you willing to spend more resources to recruit a student from a country not currently represented on campus? How is the factor of time considered when developing dual-degree programs with an overseas campus? What about retention rates, which contribute exponentially to the proverbial bottom line without expenditure of "pure" recruitment dollars in that particular fiscal year's budget?

We still have a long way to go in terms of developing such an equation. So, what can we do now to improve current metrics, to effectively justify recruitment costs to those who hold the purse strings on campus? We can take advantage of related research, and use the data as "political currency" to advance objectives during budget negotiations. It's also critical to simplify the argument whenever possible.

Calculating Recruitment Costs

Domestic admissions departments have established formulas that attempt to calculate the cost to recruit one student—the equivalent of the corporate world's "customer acquisition cost." To arrive at the per student cost, one begins by determining the return on investment (ROI) and dividing that number by the number of students enrolled from that initiative. The formula is:

$$\text{Cost to recruit one student} = \frac{\begin{array}{c}\text{ROI} = \text{(Tuition \& fees generated as a result)}\\ - \text{(Costs of recruiting initiative)}\end{array}}{\text{Number of students enrolled via that initiative}}$$

For example, one "cost of recruitment" may be the price you pay for an annual, multilingual, online promotional campaign targeting students outside of the United States. For the simple ROI formula, you would include the amount of money you pay that particular vendor, but you would not include any percentage of staff time involved in preparing the advertisement or following up with inquiries generated as a result of that effort.

Simplicity is key in this approach. Only include costs directly related to that specific recruitment effort, in effect ignoring salaries and overhead. Do not include production costs of printed material or online resources or any other costs that would have been incurred anyway, whether you engaged in this promotional activity or not. Separating the costs allows for a more accurate analysis of ROI for each initiative.

Case Studies

Here are two examples, one involving domestic travel, and the other dealing with overseas educational agents.

One colleague from the southwestern part of the United States spent $1,200 in early 2006 for a flight, hotel, and meals in D.C. for a visit to the Saudi Cultural Mission. Later that year, 20 Saudi scholarship students arrived on his campus as *a direct result of that visit—generating about $143,000 in tuition and fees, and an impressive ROI.[2]*

Most recruitment initiatives do not realize returns of such magnitude so quickly. The Saudi example is instructive, however, in emphasizing the importance of keeping the "institutional finger" on the pulse of current events and projected trends in this dynamic industry.

The second case study transpired over the course of four years starting in the early 2000s, and illuminates the industry's trend toward quality over quantity.

A U.S.-based colleague worked with an education agent in Busan, South Korea to coordinate an exclusive information session for his community college. Out of the ten students in attendance, four enrolled in English as a Second Language courses and degree programs, generating $47,840. Expenses included an agent workshop, three flights, hotels and meals, event and equipment fees, plus commissions, totaling $13,800. Return on Investment = $34,040 over four years.[3]

Obviously, this campus committed resources to enroll Korean students in particular. What is the moral of the story? The more focused your objective, the easier it is to develop a marketing strategy and measure the results. What's your ultimate goal? Do you want to fill seats with practically anyone who can afford your tuition costs? Do you want to diversify your international student population? If so, from which countries?

Quality Preferred to Quantity of Inquiries

In the past few years, international student recruiters have witnessed the transformation of the traditional wide-mouthed enrollment funnel change in shape to more of a cylinder. Colleagues now pay much more attention to the quality of initial prospects that drop into the top of the funnel, and filter down through the inquiry stage, the applicant stage, the admitted stage, and the enrolled stage. Recruiters are no longer impressed with thousands of prospective student names (generated from Web sites or fairs, for example) who probably expressed interest in hundreds of other campuses. We all want to spend resources pursuing students most likely to enroll on our particular campus, however we define the parameters of high probability.

Fortunately, technologically savvy students are also recognizing the value of fully researching their academic options prior to divulging their names and contact information to any particular campus. They understand that their data may be fed into an automated communications stream that may very well generate numerous messages. A number of education-related research studies in the United States have cited the fact that increasingly, a campus' initial contact with a prospective student is his or her actual application.

Clearly, not all inquiries are created equal. An inquiry from the sibling of a current student is obviously more valuable than most any other. Along the same lines, it's important to prioritize an inquiry from a local resident requesting more information on behalf of a friend or relative overseas. In those cases, it may be wise to forget about immediate data entry into a communications system; pick up the phone, and call the prospect as soon as possible to express your appreciation for their interest.

Market Research

One of the many advantages of the Internet lies in its capacity to conduct inexpensive market research. A global promotional campaign online can provide two types of data: 1) completed online inquiry forms, or 2) click-throughs, defined as students who view your profile on a directory site and click on your URL. The data may reveal broad geographic trends as analysts study the origin of IP addresses from the click-throughs or the countries cited in the online forms.

For example, USjournal.com noticed a significant increase in inquiries originating in Italy during the spring of 2008, even though the organization made no formal attempt to promote the site in that European region. Reasons for the trend included the favorable exchange rate of the U.S. dollar compared with the euro at the time, as well as consequences of changes in the Italian higher education system. Recognizing a trend, USjournal.com decided to launch USAcademics-it. com, an independent Italian language domain.

According to research conducted in 2008 by StudyUSA.com, about five times as many students click through to a university's Web site compared to the number who completed an inquiry form at StudyUSA.com. And considering that most students send more than one inquiry (the average is between two and three), the actual ratio is closer to ten-to-one. Clearly, measuring click-throughs is not a perfect science, as many systems do not account for "return traffic" or people who visit the university Web site subsequently and directly, without first visiting the StudyUSA site in this example.

Happily, Webmasters can track these students each time they enter, and as they travel through your site. If your site supports the technology, ask if it's possible to install "tracking codes," some of which can account for "return" traffic.

Given the enormous amount of data so easily accessible online, one challenge is to avoid "paralysis by analysis." Strike a balance between crunching reams of numbers and speaking with currently enrolled students to see how they reached their decision about where to apply. When it comes to analyzing data, pay more attention to the broader trends. For example, a widespread security breach in any particular country at any given time may result in far fewer students completing online forms; students may instead call the admissions office directly for more information.

Colleagues are becoming more sophisticated about tracking results of individual promotional campaigns by assigning a unique URL for each campaign. That approach mirrors the trend away from "broadcasting" (driving traffic to a home page, for example) toward "narrowcasting," also known as "precision marketing."

Precision Marketing

Marketers may design pay-per-click campaigns on any major search engine around the world, based on specific key words or key phrases (in any major language) and specific geographic regions (using detailed maps or points of latitude and longitude). When targeting affluent, communications-savvy users of Internet-enabled hand-held devices, marketers may also be specific about who is exposed to their message, based on the wireless carrier, device manufacturer, and/or device capabilities (such as picture-taking functions or mobile wallet capabilities). For example, a marketer may want to target German-speakers in Vienna who search for "US Universitäten" on their Siemens device that is capable of streaming video via T-Mobile.

With print advertising, a marketer can simply measure increased traffic or enrollments by creating a Web "jump" page to track response. A university in Hawaii developed a short, unique URL for their print ads. After participating for one year in two regional editions of a magazine, they were pleased with the results: more than 1,000 visits to their site.

Given the seemingly endless array of technical choices, it's important to remember the basics of sound marketing. Coordinate each element of the campaign carefully, from defining your target market, to enabling a user-friendly URL, to figuring out how to measure success. You may decide to launch a local campaign on a Chinese search engine three weeks prior to an alumni event in Shanghai. Your objective may not be lots of click throughs, but rather phone calls (to a number listed in the ad) for a local alum coordinating the event.

From Wanamaker to Ogilvy

More than 100 years ago, John Wanamaker essentially complained about the lack of data in the advertising industry. More recently, David Ogilvy (the world-renowned "father of advertising") dismissed the notion that marketing is solely a numbers game: "I notice increasing reluctance on the part of marketing executives to use judgment; they are coming to rely too much on research, and they use it as a drunkard uses a lamp post for support, rather than for illumination."

Effective international student recruitment is based more on sound judgment than on hard data. Ultimately, that's not such a bad thing when considering the complexity of global student mobility.

Endnotes

[1] Snowden, D.J.; Boone, M.E. 2007. "A Leader's Framework for Decision-Making." *Harvard Business Review,* November (p. 71) Harvard Business School Press

[2] Darrup-Boychuck, C. 2008. "Measuring Return on Investment in International Student Recruitment." *IIE Networker Magazine,* Spring, Institute of International Education

[3] Elliott, W. 2007. Request for Input: Working with Agents, *The Marketing and Recruiting Idea Factory Forum,* June 29, NAFSA: Association of International Educators Recruitment, Admissions and Preparation Knowledge Community: Marketing and Recruiting Network Discussion Forum

Resources and Networks

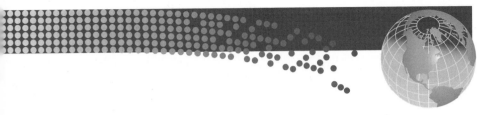

Building an On-Campus Recruitment Team

Mary Baxton

In today's competitive environment, institutions need to make use of all recruitment assistance available on their campuses in the effort to fulfill enrollment goals. We must go beyond the traditional term of outreach or admissions personnel and include faculty, staff, and students from various areas on campus. Moreover, in an enrollment management environment, we should establish and use interoffice protocols for addressing student needs among many offices on campus.

Benefits of International Recruitment Teamwork

The main benefit for international student recruitment by an on-campus team approach is the support it provides to the efforts of the offices charged with the recruiting. Making those efforts more effective and dynamic provides increased international visibility for the entire campus.

A second benefit is the opportunity to strengthen the institution's academic reputation through the involvement of faculty who are experts in their fields. No one recruiter can know the details of each major. Yet a prospective student standing with the recruiter at a fair in another country wants to know details about a proposed major. The tendency is to refer students to the major departments for more specific information from faculty who developed the curriculum and teach the courses. Staff who are knowledgeable about recruitment techniques and admission requirements are another excellent source for an on-campus recruitment team. Another component is the students and alumni who exhibit that spark of cultural diversity, good communication skills, and hold the institution in high regard.

Another benefit is the economy of scale and budget that teamwork provides. The recruitment dollars can be extended by taking advantage of faculty who are already planning to lecture internationally, or of the intensive English recruiter who is planning an extensive trip and is able to represent individual campus areas as well as the larger institution in general. Planning to attend a recruitment fair in a country where the recruiter may not know the language is the perfect opportunity to contact the alumni in that country and ask them to join you at the table. Alumni are often delighted to be called upon to assist, they can represent the institution from the student perspective, and the cost of having their assistance for the day is often minimal. At times alumni can be paired with a member of the recruitment team and then each can attend separate events in a particular country. (See Chapter 4.2: Making the Most of Alumni Contacts.)

Build the Recruitment Team

Getting Started

It is most ideal to identify one individual within the institution to serve as the team leader or a key individual when building an on-campus recruitment team. This person needs to be authorized and recognized as the team leader, and would be the point person for all aspects of team development and coordination. Much of the team structure would revolve around international admission, recruitment, and international student programs on campus, therefore the team leader should have strong knowledge in all these areas. Because there are different approaches to developing a campus recruitment team, the institution must keep in mind its role and points of strength in international education, and then identify the individual(s) who have the knowledge, passion, and drive to form the best recruitment team.

Once the leader is identified, the next step is to identify potential team members among faculty, staff, and students. A questionnaire or survey may be the most effective way to reach a potential team member and elicit information relevant to their ability to assist in recruiting efforts. The questionnaire should be preceded by a statement about the importance and relationship of international student recruitment to the strategic enrollment management and the mission of the institution.

The questionnaire should ask clear and brief questions about international travel experience, participation in international conferences, contacts abroad, current involvement with international students, marketing expertise, and interest in helping with the recruitment process. You may also want to include a list of potential recruitment activities such as:

- International travel; visiting schools overseas

- Hosting on-campus seminars on international topics for all students

- Hosting on-campus student groups involved in short-term programs

- Producing international brochures, information sheets in multiple languages, and Web content

- Attendance at regional, national, or international conferences, often presenting on international topics

- Attending college fairs in your area where potential students may be identified

- Evaluating international student transcripts to determine future transfer level and eligibility

- Networking with potential partners internationally

- Assisting with student activities such as clubs, coffee hours, weekend social functions

- Identifying current students to be used as alumni recruiters

- Interviewing prospective international students

Send the questionnaire directly to anyone you believe may in some way be able to contribute to the recruitment efforts, including faculty, administrators, department areas, staff, and students. Developing a full complement for recruitment takes time, so begin the questionnaire process as soon as possible. It will take at least six months to identify and verify members of the recruitment team. Because team members will be added and deleted over time, plan for a continual process of team building. And, finally, it is important that your potential team members understand and agree to adhere to the institution's principles of ethical recruitment before they become part of the team.

Screening and Selection

The next step is to begin the screening and selection process. Consider the skills listed below to help you determine who would be good candidates to be on the recruitment team roster.

- Overall expertise in international education

- Awareness and sensitivity to other cultures

- Ability to communicate and interact comfortably with the target audience including students, parents, counselors, and student representatives

- Experience in international travel

- Knowledge of your campus and overall programs offered

- Ability to understand the desired recruitment outcomes and results

- Knowledge of a particular major area on campus that has potential to attract international students

- Contacts in the international arena

- Foreign language skills desirable

- Recognized for attendance and presentations at regional, national, or international conferences

- Strong understanding of international admission process and academic credit evaluation

- Ability to network and build relationships with school representatives

- Good communication skills and interest in assisting with recruitment

- Willingness to be a team member on the roster for an extended period of time

Please note the importance of cultural sensitivity and the ability to understand the desired recruitment outcomes and results. You may find individuals who are experts in the field, but if they are not culturally sensitive, they will not be an effective team member. Or an individual may receive a Fulbright Scholarship and want to represent the university in the country where they are going, but they do not show a willingness to understand admission requirements or understand the desired goals of the university. You do not want a team member who may focus more on the interests of parties in the other country and suggest unreasonable concessions.

In your selection process look for colleagues who already interact with international students, faculty, and administrators with international teaching or education abroad experience; staff who understand international admission requirements and demonstrate a passion for internationalization; and current students who demonstrate the desire and abilities for recruitment.

Training Team Members

Training members of an on-campus admission team is labor intensive. With several individuals, each with his/her own experience, area of expertise, and personal schedule, it is challenging to provide the necessary training in recruitment and admissions. To help reduce the amount of individual training and guarantee consistency of training points, develop a manual that includes the following:

- A statement of recruitment goals

- Target areas and numbers of students required

- A review of available recruitment materials

- Realistic recruitment options and outcomes

- Key terms for partnerships and realistic terms of agreement

- A list of the questions most frequently asked by international students along with responses to these questions

If possible, have members visit the admissions office and take part in international student recruitment activities on campus or at local functions.

Using Team Members

Develop a recruitment team roster including name, contact information, and potential skill areas, and meet with the team members periodically. Begin an e-mail listserv.

Before they travel locally or internationally, discuss the desired goals or objectives of the trip and the format of the events in which the team member will participate. Help them prepare by summarizing your institution's relationship with the people they will be visiting, the educational structure of the country, the level of the target audience, admission requirements, and the most popular majors. Review the marketing pieces the team member will have and discuss how best to use them. Upon their return, ask them to report back to the team and note any particular outcomes, new information, and trends they observed. Map this back to recruitment materials and presentations to make sure they are hitting the mark, and place the information on the team listserv.

Briefly note the limitations of a large team approach, or perhaps better stated as know when and how to use team members. Chief among them is that team members may be volunteering their time, they may be mobile, and their availability may be limited. It may be difficult to monitor quality and measure the effectiveness of the team recruitment activity. Even with the team, international activities will take place that may not have been identified by the team. Major departments host international student groups for special events, international visitors come to the campus, or a representative visits the intensive English language office. This is part of a dynamic campus life. Difficult as it may seem, within the recruitment team, try to develop a network to identify as many of these moments as possible, and try to make the most of them. Develop a network on campus, encourage everyone to attend these events, and announce them on the listserv. Not every team member has to travel and recruit internationally or locally. They may host a number of international guests, or they may be the one who attends conferences with a focus on international issues. The ultimate success of the international recruitment team network is an increase in the number of qualified students who enroll. Monitor activity and results over at least a three-year period. Establish a benchmark by looking at the number of inquiries, applications, acceptances, enrolled students, and revenue using the chosen recruitment strategy.

Having discussed the concepts for developing an on-campus recruitment team, you must also consider building a campus support team.

Campus Support for Current International Students

Once an international enrollment goal is established and an on-campus recruitment team is formed, an ongoing group is needed to pull together the core campus functions related to international students. The organizing of this group often takes place at the same time a campus is developing a recruitment team, and it may be the same organized group on campus that comes together to begin the recruitment team. This is a working group from diverse areas across campus gathered to discuss important issues of international student enrollment, to clarify roles and processes necessary for international students from recruitment to graduation and beyond (alumni), and establish interoffice protocols for addressing student needs between offices on campus. This type of team may suggest where key functions should be housed, oversee position reviews and suggest budget and staffing increases as appropriate. This group's primary goal is to see that the functions having to do with teaching and serving international students operate in a smooth and effective fashion.

Remember Your Own Team

Lest you forget, the single most important key to success of an area is to develop your office's team. Set the example by showing a passion for international students and the work you do for them. Expect others in the area to share that belief. See that your staff have the training and skills they need so they are empowered to work with and understand your area's role in international education. Attend local, regional, and national conferences. Keep abreast of developments in the field. Know your staff and identify those who welcome the challenge. And last, if you enjoy what you do and do it well, you'll be a model for others throughout the campus community.

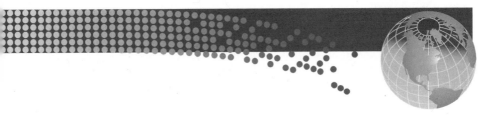

Making the Most of Alumni Contacts

Chris J. Foley

Among a school's best representatives are its students and alumni. They add a sense of authenticity to your recruitment because they can "tell it like it is." With increasing travel costs and competition among universities, your alumni can not only add a new voice to your recruitment, but they can expand your outreach immensely while reducing your costs. Alumni can be contacts "in the field," to add a friendly smile or welcoming chat over tea to an already robust recruitment plan. What's more, they provide the network that an international student will most likely need to be successful after graduation. The personal testimony, in-person outreach, and in-country network of alumni can be powerful additions to your recruitment portfolio.

Involving Alumni in International Recruiting

There are many reasons why colleges and universities involve alumni in their international recruiting. A few are listed below.

Enthusiasm

There is something very powerful about enthusiastic alumni. Word of mouth, a well-known source of domestic applications, is even more powerful with prospective international applicants. Personal relationships are a critical part of most cultures, so international students and their families pay particular attention to an enthusiastic graduate whom they already know. Moreover, admissions officers or university recruiters are often seen as "salespeople." Alumni, however, are seen as having the real "scoop" that students and their families want to hear. After all, what's more persuasive than hearing alumni talk about their university experience as the "best years" of their life?

Experience

Many alumni have overcome obstacles in going abroad and can provide inspiration to prospective applicants. They can connect the benefits of their university education with the success they had upon returning home after graduation. Offering concrete examples of their university experience and how it helped them achieve their goals is a crucial element that cannot be replicated through other means.

Networking

International alumni have an amazing network. Many have attended the same high school, are involved in the same professional organizations, and are concentrated in one or two large cities.

Credibility

Many prospective international applicants rely on spurious rankings and vague institutional reputations. Therefore, the stamp of approval from fellow countrymen and countrywomen helps reassure parents and gives them comfort in their decision to send their sons and daughters to study abroad.

Local Knowledge

Alumni can be an excellent source of local knowledge. By talking to current students and alumni you can get an inside view of their countries' economic and political situations and uncover trends that may affect your applicant pool. Alumni also know their own educational systems, can help identify selective high schools and universities, and can actually recruit at specific schools. They will often give you invaluable knowledge about influential families and the leadership potential of various candidates. International alumni can also help with logistics for the admissions officer who travels and recruits alone.

Vested Interest

Like their domestic counterparts, international alumni have a vested interest in the reputation and future of your school. They know that improving the student body adds value to their diploma.

Budget

Not every school has the budget and personnel to travel overseas to recruit. Even those who can travel can't be everywhere at once. In the absence of a staff member, alumni can represent your institution at overseas educational fairs, visit high schools, conduct student interviews, and host receptions for prospective students.

Development

Oftentimes people associate alumni with the proverbial "ask" for money, something many recruiters avoid. However, development can take many forms, and alumni are often looking for ways to give back to their institutions as a way to stay connected. Service as a recruiter is an excellent means to keep alumni interested and informed about the institution while allowing them to donate their services to the institution. An alumni recruitment program can become a central event for an alumni club, giving the alumni a cause to develop, collaborate, and become part of the glue that keeps the club together and moving forward.

Organizing Your Alumni Recruitment Program

You can organize alumni to represent your school formally or informally. Some schools use alumni on a regional basis within the U.S. and overseas, with each region having its own alumni admission representative. Others have informal alumni counselors who are listed on Web sites. Still others have admission office liaisons with each of their alumni clubs. The organizational structure of your school or department will determine which method works best for your situation.

A successful recruitment program most often happens when campus officials responsible for international student programs, alumni relations, and recruitment abroad work together and develop a coherent strategy based on international recruiting intentions, alumni presence, and institutional resources. Monitoring relations among these key groups with the help of the alumni office is well worth your time.

Here are a few tips to keep in mind as you develop your alumni student recruitment program:

- *Start small and grow.* Target one or two countries, and reach out personally to the alumni from these countries and ask for their help. Once you've had some success in these countries, add a few more each year. Identify countries that have a large number of alumni or alumni who are particularly interested in helping your institution.

- *Make sure you coordinate with your alumni association and foundation.* In many cases, these units may have fostered long-term relationships with particular alumni, and for good reasons may be very protective of these relationships. You don't want to jeopardize a situation where you undermine the foundation's efforts to obtain a large donation from any alumni.

- *Don't forget your international alumni who still live in the United States.* These alumni may not live abroad, but they often still have contacts back home and they go to visit. They may be willing to host a reception or speak to students when they go home.

- *Capitalize on energetic alumni.* If you have alumni who contact you and are willing to help you recruit students, include them if at all possible. Creating the enthusiasm for recruitment is one of the biggest hurdles. If it is already there, you're well on your way.

- *Cover as much of the cost as possible.* Recruitment is not free, and alumni recruiters will need supplies and incur costs for their activities. Don't expect alumni to foot the bill for these activities. If it is a club activity, it is often an act of goodwill to assist in covering the costs of a reception. Though alumni may refuse this assistance, the offer to help cover costs is appreciated. Also, make sure the expectations for budgets are outlined before the event. Well-meaning but overzealous alumni may put on very expensive and budget-straining events in an attempt to give a first-class recruitment event.

- *Look to your current students and recent alumni.* They have the "freshest" impression of your institution, and their interest in staying connected is probably the strongest. Try to incorporate international students into your tour guide corps or your admissions counselor staff. By training them while they are on campus, you are ensuring they'll be ready to represent you when they go back home

Alumni Records

Make sure records of permanent home addresses are correct at graduation and see that they are transferred to the alumni office. Because e-mail addresses are a more reliable way to contact alumni, be sure that you have their personal e-mail address as well as their university e-mail address. In some cases, universities allow graduates to keep their student e-mail addresses, making it much easier to stay in contact with students.

Working with Alumni Representatives

Selection

Choosing the right spokespersons is critical. Identify the characteristics you want your alumni representatives to possess, and then work closely with the international student and alumni offices to identify active alumni around the world.

Since using alumni as admissions representatives is uncommon in most countries, some admissions offices choose current students to help them by giving tours, hosting information sessions, conducting on-campus interviews, and serving on the admission committee. Such students can be your international alumni admission representatives "in training." While some universities require that alumni admissions representatives be within five years of graduation, others prefer a mix of recent graduates and older alumni who have demonstrated career success.

It is important to keep abreast of your institution's involvement in targeted regions of the world. Consider organizing on-campus regional update meetings at which admission officers, career services administrators, current international students, recent alumni, and faculty with an interest in the region get together to share knowledge and discuss potential issues related to your applicant market and recruiting strategies. This knowledge should then be shared with your alumni so they can stay "in the loop."

Training

Your volunteers must be well informed to be effective. Creating a Web page specifically for your alumni recruiters is the best way to keep all alumni informed and current. Your Web page should address the following:

- New and current academic programs
- Accomplishments of faculty
- The latest student-body profile
- Current admission policies and procedures
- Costs
- Financial aid and scholarship possibilities
- International student services
- English as a second language (ESL) programs

You may want to include a discussion on rankings, global and regional trends, or topical issues unique to your school.

Activities for Alumni Admission Representatives

In your communications, maintain the distinction between alumni who may be volunteering to help the school identify and attract prospective students, and professional institutional representatives who hold the decisionmaking power. Alumni should always be clear on what their recruitment responsibilities entail.

Alumni admission representatives can be helpful in the following activities:

- *Identifying and referring applicants.* Alumni may identify excellent candidates for your programs. Keep track of their referrals in your database. An annual report showing how alumni representatives have been helpful in the recruiting process can be invaluable and help them see the results of their work.

- *Education fairs and forums.* Alumni can provide important support at overseas education fairs. Some of the students and many of the parents may not speak English, so alumni can be extremely helpful. In many foreign countries, parents are much more involved in making college choices than are students, so it is important that their questions be answered. Professional schools may want to seek out recent graduates and high-ranking alumni to help at their booth, espousing the spirit of the current campus environment while testifying to your program's potential for success. Well-trained alumni can represent your institution at fairs that you may be unable to attend.

- *Podcasts and Web videos.* Alumni, especially recent graduates, can prepare podcasts or video presentations for prospective students. Podcasts and streaming videos are inexpensive, easy to prepare, and can be made available to prospective students via your Web site. Also, the biggest advantage is that they can be in the student's native language.

- *Information sessions and receptions.* Ask your alumni to serve as hosts for information sessions about your school. Have them partner with their company/employer to sponsor the reception, giving "name power" to your school and reception. Have your alumni talk about their university experience at secondary schools, colleges, or professional organizations. One school allows prospective students to reserve seats for such receptions via their Web site. Overseas educational advising centers and test prep centers often welcome information sessions led by alumni. (See Chapter 4.3: Developing Overseas Relationships.) Because alumni are your information disseminators, you may want to list them on your Web site, but be sure to get their permission to use their names and contact information.

- *Scholarship development and funding sources.* Alumni can develop funds that can be given to the foundation for scholarships for low-income students or other specific populations. Although few alumni are wealthy enough to endow full-ride scholarships, alumni can pool together their funding and offer small or partial scholarships at times. And even if this is not possible, alumni can be very helpful in referring students to possible sources of funding from their local governments, communities, or in-country companies. Like in the U.S., there are often funding sources within a country that are available but may not be well known, and alumni may have experience in helping students in need of funding find possible scholarship programs for which they can apply.

- *Interviews and evaluations.* The use of alumni in this area varies. Some schools prefer to standardize interviews by having their admission personnel conduct them. Others train their alumni to interview overseas. Some admission officers have alumni ask very specific questions and provide very sophisticated forms for their feedback, all communicated via e-mail. It is a curious phenomenon, but many times alumni are the most critical reviewers and provide the strongest opinions to the admission committee.

- *Assisting institutional representatives.* As previously mentioned, alumni can help by giving visiting institutional representatives valuable cultural, economic, and educational information about their country. They can also help with logistics by suggesting the best locations for events, directions to schools, and the most effective means of advertising your visit.

- *Predeparture reception.* Local alumni can help prepare new students to leave home for education at your school. Having experienced the anxiety international students feel before departure and armed with a sense of the information students need, alumni are excellent presenters at predeparture events.

The foregoing activities require different degrees of effort and levels of sophistication and budgeting. Their effectiveness, such as the predeparture send-off, may have modest budgetary implications but enormous benefits to incoming students.

Staying in Touch

Be sure to keep international alumni updated about the progress of the university. It may cost more to send mailings (newsletters, magazines, notices of regional activities) to the international alumni, but they are as interested as domestic students in the development of their alma mater. Electronic newsletters and social networking pages are becoming increasingly popular.

Universities are finding ways to reach out to their alumni, to keep the university "in front of the alumni" with the goal of keeping them attached to the university. Alumni who are "attached" are more likely to help the institution, and an alumni recruitment program is a valuable way for them to contribute.

Keep alumni informed about student applicants from their area. Tell them who was admitted and who enrolled. Their relationship with students can evolve as you progress through the admission cycle: from a provider of basic information and admission materials to a mentor as the student prepares for departure.

Working with the alumni office, keep alumni informed of other international admissions representatives through a listserv or on the alumni Web page. They like to share their experiences and learn from their fellow alumni.

Be an advocate for your alumni. Remember that a relationship developed among your alumni in their home countries can be strong advertising. Prospective applicants may be impressed with the camaraderie your alumni have developed and the pride they have in their school.

And last, be sure to say thank you. One of the most important contributions international alumni can make is an introduction of your school to future and prospective students. Be sure your campus officials recognize this as a valuable contribution and recognize the international alumni for their contributions, no matter how large or small.

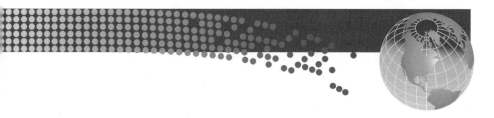

Developing Overseas Relationships

John F. Eriksen

When developing relationships overseas, an international admission office needs to consider the scope of the endeavor and understand that the process of overseas networking is never ending. Face-to-face interaction is of utmost importance, especially when building bridges across oceans, and repeated interaction strengthens the bonds. It takes time and a financial investment, but relationship building overseas can be easy, enjoyable, and helpful in recruiting international students.

In building overseas networks, an institution needs to be aware of the infrastructure already in place. The different networks that already exist are the international schools (including any secondary school that sends students overseas for education), the U.S. government (EducationUSA, U.S. Commercial Service, and U.S. Foreign Service representatives), individual colleges and universities (study abroad office or academic affairs, alumni/development office, and other globally focused departments), and third-party agents. The latter is discussed in detail in Chapter 4.4: Working with Third-Party Agents.

International Schools

The international school network is the largest in terms of the number of contacts and relationships that can be developed. These schools represent a variety of educational systems, from U.S. to Canadian to British to the International Baccalaureate (I.B.). There are also many local and public schools in which guidance/school counselors play a leading role in guiding their students to choose an institution abroad. While there is no complete list of schools that send students to the United States, there are partial lists available through the U.S. Department of State Office of Overseas Schools (www.state.gov/m/a/os/c1684.htm) and through the two membership organizations that work with the international schools: the Overseas Association of College Admission Counseling (OACAC, www.oacac.com)

and the European Council of International Schools (ECIS, www.ecis.org). Membership in these organizations is an excellent way for an institution to begin building relationships overseas.

These organizations each host an annual meeting /conference that bring together admission representatives from higher education and international school counselors, principals, and teachers. The ECIS annual conference in a European city in November and the OACAC conference on a North American campus in July each provide a great opportunity for networking with colleagues in both secondary and higher education. Conference attendees have access to a listing of institutions that actively participate in international education. Another networking opportunity is the College Board's Summer Institute for new guidance counselors at international schools. Although not as large as the international conferences, this workshop has proven to be helpful for new professionals making contacts in the field. These conferences encourage face-to-face relationship building, which is crucial to establishing an overseas network, and give the admission counselor the opportunity to contribute to and participate in the on-going professional development of counselors and admission officials.

Just as school visits are essential in domestic recruitment and relationship building, they are equally important in international recruiting efforts. Strong and meaningful working relationships are developed when an admission representative visits an international school and more importantly, meets with the school counselor and students. International admission counselors, faculty, university presidents, current students, and alumni all play an integral role in recruiting international students. With so much ground to cover, it is impossible for an admission counselor to visit every school. One way to make the most of your time in each country is to invite international school staff to lunch or dinner while you are in their country. A cup of coffee at a café goes a long way in getting to know more about the school and its students, the country, and its culture. More importantly, it gives an admission counselor a captive audience to deliver the message of the institution they represent.

Universities, colleges, and schools interested in attracting and enrolling undergraduate international students at their institutions have strong incentives to develop relationships with international schools throughout the world. Students at these schools have the most mobility and are the most globally focused within a city, country, or region. It is definitely worth an admission officer's time to work with these counselors because their students often choose U.S. universities and are proficient in English and financially capable.

The United States Government

EducationUSA

When looking at the resources provided by the U.S. government, international admission offices should start their networking with the EducationUSA offices (http://educationusa.state.gov/). EducationUSA centers are responsible for presenting nonbiased information about higher education in the United States and should serve as your primary contact for information about students, educational systems, and economic and political trends. Some centers provide specific services for U.S. institutions such as making travel arrangements, or organizing a reception and many organize college fairs and presentations throughout the country promoting education in the United States.

More than 500 advisers work in EducationUSA centers in 170 countries. They are highly trained, technologically advanced, well-informed, and innovative professionals—all good reasons for them to be strong members of your overseas network. In addition to advising students, they often administer scholarship programs and testing programs such as the SAT and TOEFL.

The EducationUSA advisers suggest that institutions place the EducationUSA logo on their international admission Web site or the campus homepage. This will provide a direct link to the main U.S. government Web site for prospective students. Also, you can develop a strong network of EducationUSA support by attending the NAFSA: Association of International Educators annual conference and hosting advisers on your campus. EducationUSA offices provide many types of support to colleges and universities and often work in conjunction with the U.S. embassy and visa officials. They counsel students who may be applying to or attending your institution and provide predeparture orientation programs for admitted students to help ease concerns about visas and offer tips for adjusting to life in the United States as well as campus life.

The EducationUSA centers are coordinated by eight Regional Educational Advising Coordinators (REACs). They are grouped geographically as follows:

- Africa
- East Asia/Pacific
- Eurasia
- Europe
- Mexico/Central America/Caribbean
- Middle East/North Africa
- South America
- South/Central Asia

The REACs primary role is as a resource for the EducationUSA advisers in their region. They provide leadership and expertise in educational advising issues to the centers and U.S. embassies, and serve as a liaison with the U.S. Department of State's Bureau of Educational and Cultural Affairs in Washington, DC.

EducationUSA can be an important partner in international recruitment along with the U.S. Commercial Service, and the two have enjoyed increased collaboration in recent years.

U.S. Commercial Service

We promote economic prosperity, enhance job creation, and strengthen national security through a global network of the best international trade professionals in the world.

We promote and protect U.S. commercial interests abroad and deliver customized solutions to ensure that U.S. businesses compete and win in the global marketplace.

The Department of Commerce U.S. Commercial Service (http://trade.gov/cs/) offers a targeted approach to building a network overseas by providing introductory meetings with overseas institutions and arranging presentations about your institution. The Commercial Service has offices in most countries around the world and is able to provide in-country support to a U.S. college/university for a nominal fee. This support can include services such as establishing contacts, scheduling meetings, providing space, and negotiating advertising rates in magazines and newspapers. While traveling in a country with a commercial service office, it can be very important for an international admission professional to take some time to meet with the staff of the office and learn how to further solidify a mutually beneficial relationship. In the United States, most states employ a liaison to the U.S. Commercial Service offices. From a time-saving and cost-effective perspective, meeting with these liaisons in an institution's home state can be an excellent opportunity.

The increased cooperation and collaboration between the U.S. Commercial Service and EducationUSA offices has been most helpful in strengthening overall promotion of U.S. education. Planning and promoting virtual fairs online, in-country education fairs and media campaigns through the internet, and traditional platforms such as radio and television are a few examples of how their collaborative efforts have improved access to education in the United States for international students.

U.S. Foreign Service

United States embassies or consulates exist in all countries of the world and are an important part of international recruitment. By meeting with consulate officials or visa officers, an institution can make known its interest in bringing international students from that country to the United States. This is especially true for colleges that are new to recruitment and/or for institutions that will begin to enroll a significant number of applicants from that country. With so many institutions of higher education in the United States, it is impossible for consular officials to be familiar with all programs. Therefore, by educating them about academic programs, recruitment efforts, and opportunities for students, an institution can prepare the way for its admitted students.

As with developing any network, communication is the key to success. The U.S. government and other governments around the world provide resources for an institution to help bring more international students to their country. The U.S. government, through EducationUSA (Fulbright), the U.S. Commercial Service, and the U.S. Foreign Service, provides important resources for an institution looking to expand its recruitment efforts overseas. International education can be quite lucrative for a country's economy. As such, governments throughout the world notice the importance of promoting and marketing education, and largely view international education as an export/import.

Working with Your Own Institution

Most institutions have international operations outside of the enrollment management office, and these offices, such as study abroad, alumni relations, career services, and others, will have contacts overseas. It is important for an institution to pool and utilize these resources when looking at building an overseas network. For example, there might be an influential alumni who can provide logistical support, information, and even marketing opportunities to help build a network overseas. Also, an international admission counselor can work with an education abroad adviser to establish contacts that can be mutually beneficial. Meeting with current U.S. education abroad students while visiting the destination country and asking them to play a vital role in recruitment is another example of institutional cooperation.

Therefore, creating an internationally focused network at an institution, in conjunction with the on-campus offices with direct or indirect involvement overseas, can help expand an overseas network. With little financial investment, an institution can combine its resources to expand its network overseas and generate familiarity with the institution throughout the world. For further details about on-campus recruitment teams, see Chapter 4.1: Building an On-Campus Recruitment Team.

Overseas Agents and Independent Counselors

More than 30 percent of U.S. institutions of higher education, along with more than 80 percent of United Kingdom and almost 90 percent of Canadian institutions, use agents. Almost all of those institutions work with independent counselors—those individuals who work with many students in local schools, both public and private, and play an important role in the college selection process for students. Usually compensated financially for their services, these counselors provide career and higher education guidance to their students. This is a great overseas network and institutions should discuss how they can best work with this group to help their recruiting efforts. See Chapter 4.4: Working with Third-Party Agents, for detailed information and guidelines.

Now What

Building an overseas network can begin immediately, and planning to attend the conferences mentioned earlier is a good way to start. Through OACAC, ECIS, and NAFSA, you can build relationships with advisers based overseas. Create a database for names of contacts around the world, and periodically e-mail or mail them updates about the institution. Also, an institution could host a number of different advisers on its campus, further developing the relationship. If an international admission office does not have the resources to travel or host international counselors, an e-mail campaign can be very successful in making these contacts. Because the high school counselor, EducationUSA adviser, teacher, or principal often has the largest impact on where a student will study, creating an overseas network is one of the strongest initiatives an institution can use to increase the number of international students on its campus.

In building an overseas network, it is important for advisers and counselors to receive accurate and fruitful information, which will help build trust in your institution. Advisers and counselors must be aware of the work that is going on in your institution, especially when it will directly impact the students they encourage to apply to the school. Advisers and counselors want to hear about the positive experiences of students and the services that are provided by your institution. To provide counselors and advisers with a true picture of your campus, it necessary for them to meet people who represent the institution, such as faculty, admission counselors, staff, or students; and through these interactions, the advisers and counselors can provide a better overview of the institution to their own students. Brochures, CDs, videos, and other media can also serve an important role in this endeavor.

In closing, institutions must be a resource for these advisers, counselors, and State Department officials, and through acting as a resource, institutions can forge strong relationships with their overseas networks. A unifying theme among advisers and counselors is the desire to establish solid working relationships with U.S. admission representatives—and to see the students they advise and counsel are well placed at American colleges and universities.

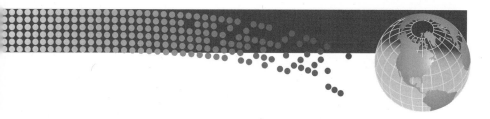

Working with Third-Party Agents

Theodore McKown II

This chapter examines the use of third-party agents or representatives by U.S. colleges and universities. For purposes of the chapter, *third-party agents* are defined as people who are not regular employees of the college or university that they represent and are compensated by commission or flat fees from a university for the specific purpose of recruiting international students for that institution. These individuals and their companies work on behalf of the institution as opposed to *educational consultants* who offer guidance and placement services on behalf of the student or the student's family.

Historically, many international education professionals in the United States believed that using third-party agents to recruit international students was a sign of weakness or poor practice. This attitude is shifting as more U.S. institutions work closely with third-party recruiters who may have greater influence within their own culture. People in other countries often see local university representatives offering a worthwhile and needed service for prospective students and their parents. At the same time, agents can become an extension of the admission office and enable the university the flexibility to cover the vast international marketplace.

Contracting with a third party to represent your university is ethical as long as the agent's representation is consistent with good recruitment principles and practices as outlined in the current NAFSA Statement of Ethical Principles, www.nafsa.org/ethics. The agent, in essence, becomes an extension of the university and should be trained about its programs, admission requirements, and selling points to name a few items. The important point when forming relationships with agents is to check their references and understand the quality of students they represent.

A major difficulty for institutions in the United States has been determining which agents are legitimate and reputable. Utilization of agents can prove to be effective but it also carries a lot of risk as the reputation of the U.S. institution is on the line. Collaboration with other institutions can limit the amount of risk and provide a sense of ethical consciousness.

Consortiums of universities are becoming an alternative as universities pool their agents for verification and consistency. For example, the public universities in Ohio are beginning to make utilization of agents across colleges a common practice through the Ohio International Consortium, giving the university more weight when problems arise and administration comfort in the screening process of these agents. This model can be used in many settings across the United States.

Most agents have an interest in doing a reputable job of learning about U.S. education and your institution, and advising the student competently. Some, however, may be running a travel agency and offer advising merely to get prospective travelers into the travel office. In other words, agents' credentials vary as widely as the services they perform and their status within the institution. In some countries, specifically Australia and India, agents have their own organizations and networks, and are developing professional standards.

Who Uses Agents and Why?

The most commonly stated reasons for using third-party recruiters are cost effectiveness and maintaining enrollment levels. Most institutions cannot afford to recruit in all markets simultaneously or in the variety of countries from which they want to receive students. However, using agents requires universities to spend resources for marketing and does not replace a recruitment budget. It is a way in which funds can be allocated efficiently. Using third-party recruiters has proved beneficial for institutions that give the practice adequate thought, establish cogent guidelines, and treat third-party recruiters as contract employees.

When an institution has experienced a decline in enrollment, with attendant budget problems, international students are one of several audiences that may be designated for increasing enrollment. Likewise, when a campus is internationalizing or "globalizing," international student enrollment may be identified as an institutional priority. For example, the university may wish to diversify enrollment. Third-party recruiters may be the most effective way to recruit students from many areas around the world, but they are prevalent in Asia, Latin America, and the Middle East.

Agents living in the target country know the local environment better than recruiters who visit occasionally. Such agents become a continuous presence in the environment and represent the institution year-round. Institutional travel is essential to enhance the agent's activity. An agent can provide information to students on an on-going basis and can supply the institution with leads throughout the year. However, an agent's scope of authority to act on behalf of the university must be clearly defined and monitored. The agent must be trained to understand program offerings and selling points of the university.

In the above circumstances, an institution may consider using a third-party recruiter in conjunction with other regular international recruitment activities to increase or stabilize its enrollments from certain parts of the world. Agents, however, do not replace the need for the university representative to travel. The admission specialist must travel to be the face of the university and establish a presence in the market as well as train the agent on programming, policies, and procedures of the university (see Chapter 4.1: Building an On-Campus Recruitment Team).

Disadvantages of Using Agents

On occasion, using an agent can become a public relations nightmare. One or two misunderstandings may hurt your institution's reputation in following years. Therefore, it's important to understand some of the possible disadvantages, such as:

- Agents can be more expensive than anticipated and the costs may be hard to contain.

- You will not learn as much about the local educational, cultural, economic, or social environment of target regions if you do not visit regularly.

- Agents may give students incorrect information. Regular contact via the Internet and travel can help solve this problem. A training manual should be developed and semi-annual trainings are important.

- Agents may make promises that cannot be delivered. Local cultural and political pressures may cause agents to overstate what they can deliver.

- Agents may commit fraud, such as overstating the cost of attending your institution, collecting the money, and retaining the difference between the amount owed and the amount collected—or worse, abscond with the whole amount.

- Agents may ask to be your "exclusive representative" in a given city or country. The agency may spend money promoting the university and want credit for eventual placements even if it did not refer them personally.

Finding a Reliable Agent to Represent Your Institution

If you want to use agents to recruit international students, you must invest the time required to find a reputable agency. If you have identified particular countries on which to focus, it may be worthwhile to visit them to locate an agent. The advantage of meeting agents in this way is that you can see their place of business, see how they present other universities, check out computer facilities, and query them at length on their knowledge of U.S. higher education and your institution. You should also seek local references. Local counselors and advisers may be able to make introductions and help you narrow the field.

As you interview prospective agents, ask them to identify the number of other institutions for whom they are working. What criteria would make them refer a student to your institution rather than another institution or vice versa?

You will want to know the local labor laws for each country in which you are hiring personnel. Some countries may have labor regulations quite different from those of the United States. If you offer employment to someone, are you subject to that country's laws? In one case, after an individual was employed for 12 months by a U.S. university, that country's law required that the university keep that person as an employee for life.

It is a good idea to limit the number of countries in which you use an agent to minimize management time and reduce the risk of a negative incident resulting from insufficient oversight. It is recommended you use a few agents in a particular region but do not use too many. When this happens an agent will limit the number of leads you receive and will funnel more leads to institutions that have stronger commitments to that agent.

Some international conferences and organizations host workshops that bring together educational advisers, referral and travel agents, and university representatives. ICEF (www.icef.com) regularly organizes workshops in locations such as Miami, for South American contacts, and Hawaii, for Asian contacts.

WHAT AGENTS CAN AND CANNOT DO

Agents can:

- Distribute your materials on a regular basis to local candidates.
- Place advertising in local papers on your behalf, particularly in the local language.
- Give you advice on what majors local students are currently seeking.
- Assist you in finding sources of students in underrepresented majors.
- Arrange appointments for you when you visit.
- Gather students for you to see when you visit.
- Learn about your certificate, diploma, and degree programs and admission requirements, as well as represent you in the local environment.

Agents cannot:

- Make admission decisions or promise admission to particular programs.
- Issue Department of Homeland Security (DHS) and Department of State (DOS) forms needed by students to obtain a U.S. visa.
- Collect money from the student for tuition and fees.
- Overstate or misrepresent their authority on your behalf.

Agents like to represent a group of universities within a particular geographic region or state. This allows them access to multiple university types and program offerings. It is recommended to partner with other institutions in your area to allow this variety for the agent. Working with other universities in your area can help in reviewing and monitoring the reliability of the agent. There is more at stake if the agent makes an unethical decision because the relationship with the consortium of institutions may be jeopardized.

The American International Recruitment Council (AIRC) was established in June 2008 to develop standards of ethical practice for agents working with U.S. institutions and to provide training for institutions that want to work with agents overseas. The goal of the council is to serve as a place where agents can go to receive certification. In turn, U.S. institutions will be able to view a list of reputable agents who have met the standards of the council. This service is now in its infancy, but more information can be found on the AIRC Web site at www.airc-education.org.

Managing an Agent Relationship

Managing agents requires a lot of time. An effective recruitment program requires that you not only respond to your agents' communications but that you guide and direct their activities so that you get needed results. Managing agents can consume other resources: costs for services such as international telephone calls and faxes, computer access, and mailing costs can add up. Be sure to budget for these items.

- Meet with agents annually, either on your campus or in their country. Encourage them to visit your campus as often as possible, at your expense or theirs, so they can describe to prospective students the environment, academic programs, and people. Agents will represent you much more competently from first-hand experience rather than from information gleaned from a book.

- Provide agents with training about your programs, procedures, and policies. Keep them supplied with current materials. As far as possible, treat them as members of your staff who need regular communication.

- Call agents several times per year to develop your relationship, inquire after their business, and assess the prospects for referrals to your programs.

- Use a database to monitor the terms of contracts made with agents.

- Have the contract reviewed by knowledgeable legal representatives.

- Establish a system for tracking referrals from agents to eliminate or at least minimize conflicts over compensation. If you cannot produce information from your system about how many referrals you received from an agent, you will have difficulty resolving disagreements over compensation. Computer monitoring will help you assess the success of the contract. If an agent produces no results, the database will help determine when it is time to make a change.

- Be clear about how money is to be handled. Do not authorize representatives to collect money on your behalf, but realize that such restriction may be hard to control, particularly if you do not have a formal contract with the representative. Do everything possible to ensure that students or their families remit tuition payments directly to your institution. At the very least, make sure students know the amount of tuition and fees required for enrollment. Students have appeared at institutions claiming to have paid tuition to an agent who cannot be found. If collection of money is involved, be sure an audit trail is in place.

An exception to the preceding rule may be made when agents have recruited a group of students to travel together to your institution. Under such circumstances, require the agents to differentiate clearly between their fees, your institution's tuition and fees, travel expenses, and other costs.

Tips on International Contracts with Foreign Representatives

When signing contracts with agencies that may want to represent your institution overseas, there are many things to keep in mind. The list that follows is by no means complete, but it will raise your awareness of items to be considered before the contract is written.

- The term *agent* may imply a degree of contractual legal authority that goes beyond what you want to grant. You may want to find a term that does not imply such authority and require that the individuals who represent you overseas use that term in introductions. *Representative* may be less authoritative.

- Take care to specify and limit the ability of your representatives to make legally binding commitments on behalf of your institution. Otherwise, you may find yourself responsible for your representative's purchases.

- Spell out in detail what the agent can and cannot do. For example, agents may disseminate your brochures and catalogs; pass the client name to you; advise the client on application procedures, registration procedures, fee structure, program content, and registration dates. Agents must not promise or imply that they can secure admission to degree programs and should not handle the completed application, receive the application fee, or collect tuition.

- What are your institution's responsibilities in the contract? How often will you provide refreshed data? In what quantities will you provide information? How should the agent secure more of your literature? How frequently will you contact the agent?

- Agree on how referrals will be identified and at what point or when you pay for them.

- Ideally, you should obligate yourself to pay only for enrollees, and not for lists of names or for applicants. It is recommended that all activity from a specific area be filtered through the agency to limit confusion.

- Make sure the contract can be terminated at your discretion at any time. Be sure the contract's termination clause specifies the residual obligations of the representative; for example, to return materials and equipment, prepare final reports, pay outstanding bills and taxes, remit financial statements, and so on.

- Specify the level of training you will provide for your representative. How often will the agent receive training and at whose expense? Who will provide it and where?

- Be sure to identify any reimbursable expenses in the contract.

- Specify the equipment you expect agents to have and assign responsibility for related bills (such as telephone bills, Internet access, and computer supplies).

- Establish marketing goals and set priorities. Will the agent market intensive English programs first? Master degrees rather than bachelor degrees? diplomas rather than or before certificates? Spell out what will happen if the agent does not meet the defined goals. Will he or she receive partial payment for goals partially met or be terminated if not successful? Be sure the contract is clear.

- Specify the nature, frequency, and form of the reports you require from the agent. By what means will reports be transmitted? Identify the consequences of failure to deliver promised reports.

- Have the contract reviewed by a lawyer in the agent's country. A contract executed in the United States may not be binding.

- Specify how the agent will be paid (in U.S. dollars or local currency, by check, or by bank transfer) and how often. Make sure you know whether your institution will incur a U.S. or foreign tax liability.

- If you must pay an agent in local currency, be sure your institution is familiar with exchange rates and monetary exchange procedures. Someone in the office should monitor the exchange rate fluctuations as they can greatly affect your budget. Ask your bank how to make a wire transfer, and consider establishing an account in an international bank for the agent so you can deposit money directly to his or her account. Establish a reserve for currency fluctuations.

- Specify how you will determine when the student has been successfully recruited. How long must the student study with you before you compensate the agent? one week? one term? one semester? What happens to the agency fee if the student drops out and gets a refund of tuition? If the agency has collected the tuition and paid the fees, who gets the refund?

Compensating Agents

Compensation for agents varies greatly from institution to institution and even within institutions; i.e., from academic programs to intensive English language programs. When compensation is arranged, questions arise. Are there layers of reward to be earned?

Should agents receive the same compensation for each enrollment, or should they be paid on a graduated scale? Should you require a minimum number of enrollments before any fees are due? Will you provide a bonus for extraordinary results?

Many public institutions in the United States are prevented by law from contracting with individuals outside the United States (or outside their state, for that matter) without layers of permission. Under such circumstances, a prospective agent may suggest compensation in the form of payment of expenses such as those for the agent's travel or ads the agent places that also benefits the university. An agent may propose to make referrals to an institution in exchange for assistance in placing a particular student in a particular program, hosting a dignitary, or, indeed, hosting the agent during U.S. travel. Institutions are advised to negotiate such arrangements with care. A good, solid relationship built over years between the agent and institutional representatives can work quite well.

Some institutions retain agents by offering a certain amount of money over a certain period of time to locate qualified individuals, without specifying a precise number of students to be recruited. Such retainer arrangements ease the pressure of "head-count" compensation and place the emphasis on finding qualified individuals. If the applications you receive are insufficient in quality or quantity, the retainer is not renewed. Under retainer arrangements, agents perform a specific job for the institution within certain parameters and with certain expected outcomes.

Some institutions agree to pay agents a percentage of the tuition paid to the university. If this arrangement is chosen, determine whether the agent gets paid for subsequent semesters of enrollment or just for the first. Another model is compensation for the number of students recruited. Both models require careful definition; both are ripe for scams. Agents operating under such arrangements may be motivated to seek head count rather than qualified students. Institutions are cautioned to specify the exact conditions for payment (e.g., upon the student's enrollment). If the institution does not do so, it can expect frivolous applications and troublesome claims from the agents who generated them.

Long-Term Success

Many institutions report satisfactory arrangements with agents abroad. Success is usually proportional to planning, management, communication, and commitment. The best relationships are built on trust, respect, and competence. After careful selection, incorporate the representatives as part of your on-going recruitment planning and let them know that you are interested in a long-term relationship. It is the "long-term" that makes working with agents worthwhile.

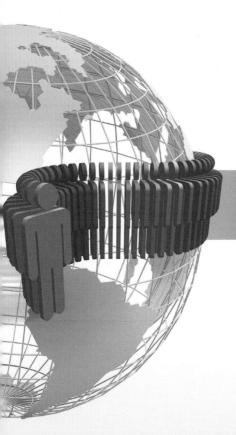

Special Programs

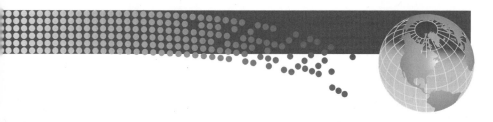

Intensive English Programs

S. Kelly Franklin

The most important advice for Intensive English Program (IEP) staffers looking for information is: read the rest of this book. The essentials of international recruiting are much the same across the spectrum of institution types, in terms of developing an infrastructure, researching markets, and considering advertising options.

This chapter outlines the differences in recruiting for universities and IEPs, and between stand-alone programs and university-based programs. It offers information and advice about various methods for reaching prospective IEP students and expanding intended markets.

A large portion of recruiting methodology holds universally, but it's nonetheless important to analyze carefully each school's situation. Recruiting for an IEP connected to a famous university in a world-famous city is quite different than recruiting for an IEP unknown outside its region, much less the country. Oftentimes, recruiting gurus who honed their craft working at large, well-funded schools in major cities have trouble grasping the challenges existing at small, unknown programs with shoestring budgets.

Differences Between IEPs and Universities

Universities make a choice as to whether to recruit international students because most would survive regardless of international numbers, whereas recruiting internationally is the lifeblood and sine qua non of existence for most IEPs. The survival of virtually every IEP depends on being aware of marketing issues, current and potential student flow patterns to the United States, and the economic and political conditions that affect recruiting outcomes.

Universities are concerned with the quality of their applicant pool, whereas most IEPs are looking for high numbers of applicants and do not emphasize academic background. IEPs need students who speak different languages and come from various countries. Peter Schilling, recruiting coordinator for the Center for English Language and Orientation Programs (CELOP) at Boston University, points out that while diversity is nice for a university, "diversity of languages is more important to the ESL classroom than to Math 110, so reaching ESL students in many countries is critical." Diverse populations make for happier students and teachers, look better to prospective clients, and help avoid enrollment drops because of sudden changes within one feeder country. IEP veterans remember when programs existed thanks to Iranians and Venezuelans, then to Japanese, and more recently, Koreans and Saudis. Putting all the eggs into any one basket, and not diversifying, spelled doom for some programs and could do the same in the future.

Unlike universities with fixed terms, IEPs often have greater flexibility to set their calendars and term length. They can tweak their schedules to have two or three start dates within one semester. Schools should make careful decisions on program length and contact hours per week to suit the markets they pursue and feel most positive about attracting. Short-term programs, such as from four to seven weeks, may be more suitable for vacationing students or others wanting general English, while longer semester-length programs may be more attractive to those seeking academic preparation or those who have received conditional admission from parent universities. If short-term programs are planned, dates and lengths should align with the educational systems and vacations of desired markets. While setting up program lengths, schools should also examine pedagogical implications to avoid promises of overly ambitious language gains; guarantees of rapid improvement over short periods, once unmet, will eventually yield negative results from unsatisfied customers.

Another area of difference is in the speed of response and processing times. Some universities can be slow to respond and still fill all seats with the students of their choice. For most IEPs, quick turnaround is essential. Students often remark that they chose their IEP based on which school replied to them first. Agents much prefer schools that respond quickly and completely and get I-20s out fast. The cost of express courier service and extra personnel to speed up processing is a well-advised, long-term investment.

IEP marketers should cooperate with their university's existing recruiting partners, such as exchange/sister schools, foreign embassies, NGOs, etc., and also explore their own connections with sponsoring program agencies, which often have two sets of contracted/referred schools—one for academic programs and another for IEPs. Such programs can bring in revenue and students from under-represented areas, again giving added diversity. Significant price cuts or cost sharing with these agencies can often pay off with long-term dividends; the same is true for price reductions or scholarships in any market strongly coveted. While offering scholarships can be tricky, if an IEP can find an appropriate partner in target countries, such as willing overseas education advising offices, the short-term financial loss *can become beneficial* by introducing the program to new potential students and especially if the recipients return home happy.

IEPs should not neglect potential customers who are not typical university-age, single-applicant students, such as lucrative holiday season short-term programs for group travel/study tours (in both northern and southern hemisphere "summer" periods). Another short-term program may be designed for middle school students in Korea and Taiwan. Other possible select groups could include local immigrant populations, nearby industries with high numbers of non-English speaking workers, and even local K-12 ESL programs.

Stand-Alone Compared to University-Based IEPs

Private, stand-alone IEPs have special conditions affecting their recruitment success. May Arthur, North American Director of Business Development for EC English Language Schools, says that private, stand-alone schools must think much like real estate agents, stressing "location, location, location." Most stand-alone IEPs are in large cities and promote their exciting urban areas. Private schools may also find niche markets and rapidly tailor their offerings to suit special circumstances. They should promote their flexibility in working with agents and contract partners to develop special programs, pricing, and payment structures.

While stand-alone schools cannot promote their university affiliations, they may be able to go one step beyond and develop ties and articulate agreements with many institutions. Stand alones may be more willing and able to set up consortia of fellow English schools or develop connections with a wider range of other education sources. They do not have to limit their focus to academic institutions but can explore vocational training opportunities that appeal to a wider range of potential students and agents overseas.

One infrastructure issue not specific to stand alones, but surely more prevalent with them, is that of housing. According to David Anderson, director of university admissions and recruitment for ELS Language Centers, providing suitable housing is important enough that proprietary (private) schools "may need to bite the bullet and take on that high, fixed cost."

Proprietary schools should also consider the cost of accreditation by the Accrediting Council for Continuing Education and Training (ACCET, www.accet.org/) or the Commission on English Language Program Accreditation (CEA, www.cea-accredit.org/). Assuming CEA accreditation becomes well-known worldwide or government regulations change to mandate accreditation for I-20 issuance, many schools will take a large "hit" on their available resources to cover this necessity. Currently, accreditation in and of itself may not be seen as a necessary expense, but market perceptions may change so that not being accredited can become a recruiting black mark.

University-based schools cannot assume that their affiliation alone ensures adequate selling strength. They often provide housing, and other services (food service, health care, sports events and facilities, plus other student-related programming) and student transition from ESL to academic studies. Therefore, university-based schools should trumpet the integration of ESL students into the full social fabric of the host institution. Marketing material and "stump speeches" should clearly define routes for the IEP student to matriculate to university programs, and stress the programs they provide (such as Conversation Partners or activities mixing internationals with all students on campus, especially American) to help their students feel like "regular" members of the community.

Conditional admissions policies are especially appealing to students and agents overseas. Such policies allow potential students to apply and be accepted to academic degree programs without English proficiency scores on standardized tests. While proprietary schools can develop tie-ins and articulation agreements, the ability of a student to be granted full acceptance to their first choice school, then improve their English either before or after arrival, is a strong selling point for university IEPs. Similarly, schools that can develop bridge or hybrid programs, in which students of a certain proficiency can begin academic coursework while completing necessary English training, have a distinct advantage over "all or nothing" approaches for student matriculation into academic programs. Many IEP students have "test phobia," so IEPs might develop alternative assessment methods for proficiency, such as portfolios or teacher recommendations. Schools with such policies would be wise to develop, define, and highlight these benefits. Simply assuming that potential clients will see "sharing space with a university" as enough of a benefit is unwise.

Basics of Materials Development

It seems obvious, but a cursory look at even a handful of different schools' brochures or Web sites will usually show that this point bears repeating: the select audience, in most cases for IEP materials, is non-English readers. Materials should be simple and direct, with no idiomatic phrasing. Even high-level non-native English speakers can be stumped by phrasing that may seem obvious to natives. One simple example was when a graduate student in a TESOL program from China (with very strong English skills) asked this writer what their institution was referring to when it promoted the fact that a national magazine had called it a "hot" school. Living in upstate New York, she had not thought of the school in those terms, climatologically speaking, and had no other definitions of "hot" as applied to a university in her lexicon.

IEPs should not depend on outside marketing gurus for material and picture content, unless the marketers have extensive experience dealing with international and non-native English speaking markets (and even then....what international market? Requirements can vary greatly across and even within continents). The domestic audience is often swayed by "soft" images that don't convey specific details, whereas potential customers overseas tend to need and want more specific information in text and pictures. They want to see a dormitory room and know what furniture will be there, and they want to know the exact class schedule or precise fees beyond basic tuition. They demand and deserve concrete details.

Materials of any type should be translated into as many languages as possible. Vocabularies in the same language can vary from region to region (Spanish and Chinese especially), thus it is worth the extra cost to get professional translators or students with a strong command of the languages and with marketing savvy to understand not only what to say but how to say it. Just as English speakers chuckle over poor translations coming from other countries, the school's image could be tarnished considerably from poor translations.

Print Materials

Many recruiters no longer send brochures to inquiries, unless specifically requested, or when trying to reach a specific market. However, print materials are still needed for partners, agents, advising centers and college fairs.

The weight of materials must be considered, since they will be mailed, shipped or carried overseas. Extra care should be taken in dealing with the printers, who again, are attuned to domestic-program needs and have not thought about such issues as how thin paper stock can be without bleeding ink from front to back sides.

University-based IEP recruiters would be wise to review their universities' road pieces, and either create separate international pieces or supplements that discuss issues germane to internationals that are often glossed over or missing from domestic-centered materials. Similar principles hold true with application forms; pare down the information requested to the minimum required for completing the process and issuing an I-20. Because most applicants who can afford IEP attendance have e-mail access, schools should consider moving all communication and information-gathering to e-mail exchanges following the acceptance and I-20 issuance. These e-mail exchanges are also beneficial ways to help strengthen the tie between school and student prior to arrival.

Web Sites

The site address should be easy to type, easy to find (university programs may have a disadvantage here, being limited to what the university Webmasters will allow for placement, address conventions, etc.), and include the information needed to answer basic questions and accept an application. "The Web site, and driving traffic to that site, is the most critical piece to recruiting ESL students" says Schilling of CELOP.

Print Ads

If ads are in English, will your select audience of non-English readers bother with them? Where will potential clients see the ads? One recruiter commented that the only place he ever saw his school's ads in one publication was in the US consular section waiting rooms, where people would see it as they waited for their visa interview to attend another school—not prime time for exposure!

Print ads may have some value when entering a new market, developing name recognition, or if they are inexpensive. Otherwise, since most print ads are expensive and reach a small market, Anderson of ELS says simply, "Print ads are never the answer for ESL programs."

Web Ads

"The verdict is still out on the overall effectiveness of on-line ads," says Schilling, but a few strategically placed and inexpensive ads may enhance a school's presence in selected markets. When deciding on using a third-party Web advertiser, schools should explore how and where the site is promoted, and how inquiry information will be delivered. (See the checklist, What to Consider Before You Advertise, in Chapter 3.1: Advertising: What, Where, and When to Say It.)

Care should be given to how schools are listed. Will your school be listed alphabetically (good for Alabama, not for Ypsilanti), or by region? The cost of the ads must be weighed against the number and quality of leads. Savvy marketers can lead many internet users to their site and gimmick them to inquire, but are they leading inquiries to you from those who already have sufficient English or don't have money or can't get visas?

Recruitment Fairs

While some ESL recruiters believe that the hey-day of fairs and their ability to reach markets and students has passed, a fair remains valuable in many cases and can serve as the linchpin for visits to countries where fairs are still common. For a broad discussion of recruitment fairs, see Chapter 3.3: Recruitment Fairs. For IEPs specifically, knowing how and where the fair is promoted is important; some are advertised mainly in English-only newspapers, in international schools or advising centers that focus more on university admissions, for example.

Physical groupings of schools by fair organizers may be of higher importance to IEPs. For example, does a university-based program want to be lumped together with other IEPs or with universities? Is it better to participate in a fair promoting U.S.-based schools or to be mixed with schools from around the world? Is a fair attended by high schools and vocational schools from around the world more beneficial than one exclusively for higher education clients?

Schools new to fairs often waste money by not following "the three-year rule" observed by many veterans. Schools should not expect fairs to yield immediate results unless they are well known, offer something unique and highly desired and/or provide exceptionally good value for money.

IEPs should consider the use of translators at fairs. Many university-bound students want to visit with school officials to show off their language prowess and push their case for acceptance, while potential ESL students may be happier to talk with translators or former students to learn the nitty gritty details of life at the school. Traveling to meet students is less of a priority for IEPs than for degree programs, since students are more likely to search for a program on-line or follow friends' recommendations. "Choosing an ESL program is less daunting and carries fewer implications than finding the right degree program, so students seeking ESL are less likely to feel the urgent need to meet the school rep at a fair," Schilling says.

Recruitment and Third-Party Agents

The good news is that most people involved in the international recruiting arena are realizing that in many countries, the use of agents is virtually unavoidable. Smart recruiters know in which countries they need to make these connections and in which countries it is more advisable to avoid them. Both situations clearly exist. In any case, the key is in knowing that good and useful agents can be counted on to be honest with recruiters, prospective students, and their parents.

Although many agents prefer university programs that have straight connections, there is clearly a market in many countries for the type of programs that promote the vacation side of study abroad more than study itself. So, stand-alone IEPs in popular vacation spots can have good success working with third-party recruiters.

Since working with agents is broadly covered in Chapter 4.4: Working with Third-Party Agents, here are just a few tips:

1. Set up a good system to get and keep information on agents and to record the number of students received and commissions paid.

2. Consider carefully commission amounts. Schools should know what the market can bear, what is standard, and what they need to offer to get agents to refer students to them. Different countries may merit different commission rates.

3. Visits to agents are useful both to present your information and to check out their businesses. In some countries, setting up an agency is extremely easy and done with little expertise or financial backing. It is valuable to see for yourself if an office exists, if students are finding it, and if the person giving advice has any idea about what they are promoting.

4. Develop materials specifically for agents that put in one place all key information, but be prepared for them to ignore the manuals and contact you with endless e-mails and extensive one-size-fits-all surveys.

Getting contact information of agencies becomes easier daily with Web access and the proliferation of agency associations within countries, regions and even worldwide. Start with the Federation of English Language and Consulting Association, www.FELCA.org. In addition, agent workshops, in which an organizing firm brings together schools and agents in a "speed dating" type of format, can introduce a school to 30-40 agents in a few days without excessive travel. Although the upfront cost is high, workshops can bring instant results. If considering workshops, schools should discern, if possible, what agents are attending and should be clear on their own policies regarding commissions and level of representation they want from the agents.

Schools with more resources or with good consortia arrangements with other institutions may want to arrange familiarization ("fam") tours for a number of agents to see the school and environs firsthand. This is more common in the

United Kingdom and other countries that don't face the geographical limitations in the United States, but the visits can be effective if costs are reasonable. Even schools that generally do not pay commissions may find them useful in selected countries, especially if the school is new to the market or wants to increase diversity.

Even schools that do not offer payment to agents should keep in mind that working with third parties can be beneficial. Some agents do not accept commissions, but work from student fees and charge their clients for admission to the best possible schools (not only top-flight schools, but sometimes the best school for that particular person). Most IEPs also find it useful to develop ties for receiving students with international businesses in their area, overseas language schools and educational institutions, and other external organizations. In other words, as Schilling says, "Solid partnerships over the long term can be a buffer against hard times (like post 9-11)."

Alumni

While covered extensively in Chapter 4.2: Making the Most of Alumni Contacts, the use of IEP alumni should be encouraged. It's well worth keeping in touch with them via newsletters or other social networks, so they can be tapped for support. Having alumni who are knowledgeable about the host country and your school available at fairs, online or by telephone, to answer the questions and calm the fears of potential students and parents, can pay off handsomely. Often the alumni base of an IEP is more engaged and on closer terms with the staff that visits their country than would be the case for recent university graduates who might not have met admissions counselors. Also, dinners or other social functions that bring alumni together often lead to new connections and ultimately to more students.

Stay Up-to-Date

It is worth repeating that IEP recruiters should read and study this entire book, pick the brains of veterans, and use all resources possible, while at the same time remembering that their specific institution will have unique needs, challenges and successes. Similarly, time situations, generations, and countries change. An effective type of recruitment today in country X may not work tomorrow in that same country or more so, in country Y. Good recruiters continually study the environment, the competition, and also their own programs to remain successful.

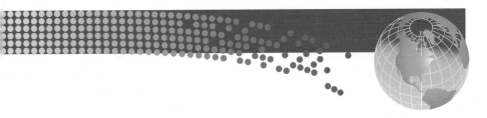

Community Colleges

Eddie West

There are more than 1,200 regionally accredited community colleges in the United States. More than 11 million students are learning at these schools, nearly half of all undergraduate students in the United States. Most community colleges came into existence to serve the local population. Today, however, these institutions are actively broadening their student bodies to include international students. According to the 2007 Institute of International Education (www.iie.org) *Open Doors* report, 86,179 international students were studying at community colleges during the preceding academic year. This figure represents a 22 percent increase since the year 2000. By way of comparison, the total number of international students in the United States grew just 13 percent, to 582,984 students, during this same seven-year period.

This chapter describes the strengths you can highlight to attract international students to your community college. It also examines the challenges you may face as you begin your outreach efforts and how to overcome them, and concludes by outlining specific recruitment strategies that have been used successfully by community colleges in the United States.

Advantages of the U.S. Community College

Low Tuition Costs

Most international students and their families appreciate the relatively low cost of U.S. community college tuition. International students studying at U.S. community colleges typically pay higher tuition and fees than do American students at the same schools. However, in most cases "nonresident, noncitizen" tuition rates at community colleges are considerably lower than those at four-year schools. International students intending to obtain a bachelor's degree in the United States can save many thousands of dollars in tuition by completing their first two years of study at a community college.

University Transfer

Each year many international students transfer from community college to a four-year university. And like their U.S. counterparts, many international students choose to begin their study at a community college in no small part because of this very transfer possibility. A school-to-school transfer system is uncommon in the higher education system of most other countries. The "2 plus 2" system, as it is sometimes called, is therefore a particularly strong selling point for community colleges that can offer such opportunities to international students.

Small Classes

Community college class sizes tend to be smaller than large public university classes. Introductory general education courses at large public universities often have enrollments of hundreds of students. By contrast, class sizes at most community colleges seldom approach that size. In most instances, student-faculty ratios at community colleges are significantly lower than those at four-year schools.

Teaching and Learning Focused

Community college faculty focus on teaching or, put differently, on facilitating students' learning. While many community college faculty engage in research and other scholarly pursuits, these are separate undertakings beyond their full-time instructional commitment. This contrasts with the situation at research universities, where "publish or perish" is the name of the game for faculty seeking tenure or other forms of advancement. Also, community college courses are rarely taught by graduate students or teaching assistants.

Flexible Language Requirements

English language admission policies at many U.S. community colleges are relatively flexible, especially when compared with some of the strict requirements at four-year colleges and universities. Most community colleges boast preparatory English as a Second Language (ESL) coursework to help international students improve their language proficiency. Some colleges offer intensive English language programs for international students needing basic language instruction and/or who are interested in improving their English more quickly.

Test Of English as a Foreign Language (TOEFL) admission requirements tend to be lower at community colleges than at four-year universities. Students who are particularly eager to begin degree-program studies in the United States are often drawn to this lower barrier to higher education entry that is found at the community college level.

Optional Practical Training (OPT) and Curricular Practical Training (CPT)

Like four-year universities, community colleges approved by the Student and Exchange Visitor Program (SEVP) afford qualified international students the opportunity to engage in Optional Practical Training (OPT) and Curricular Practical Training (CPT). Students can consult with their Designated School Official (DSO) about the availability of practical training during and after completing an associate degree program. They can also talk with their DSO about the availability of additional OPT after transferring to a four-year university.

Recruitment Challenges and How to Neutralize Them

Lack of Familiarity with the Community College Model

Most Americans are well aware of the community college and its place in the broader realm of U.S. higher education. The same cannot be said in most other countries in the world. Some countries, like Japan and Canada, have their own established system of two-year schools, and so comfort with the U.S. community college system tends to be relatively high among those students and their families. Other countries, such as India and China, do not have a common, comparable institutional model. Therefore, the concept of the U.S. community college—including its transfer relationships with four-year universities—is terra incognita.

Community college officials responsible for international outreach should be aware of these distinctions and recognize that many students and their families need to be educated about the model and nature of the U.S. community college. The American Association of Community Colleges (AACC) has some excellent materials on this subject.

Perception That Low Tuition Costs Equals Low Quality

The low cost of U.S. community college tuition may come as a surprise to potential international students and their parents. One would assume that it would be a pleasant surprise, but for some, the relatively low tuition of the community college may arouse suspicion that "low cost equals low quality." As a result, these individuals may not seriously consider the option of applying to a community college.

You can address this concern by communicating the unique value of the community college and explaining why its costs to students can be lower than those at universities. You may explain that the first two years of undergraduate education consist primarily of general education and introductory-level courses whether a student begins at a community college or at a university. As such, equipment and facilities needs are not as great as they are for upper division and graduate-level coursework, so this helps keep the cost of community college tuition relatively low. Also, because community colleges are not engaged in pure or applied research as part of their core mission, research and development costs are also not part of the equation.

Lack of On-Campus Housing

Because most community colleges lack on-campus housing for their students, this issue needs to be addressed forthrightly. Most prospective international students do not have friends or relatives near their new school, and it is not easy for them to secure off-campus housing while still in their home countries. They will need assistance.

Schools can address this by dedicating staff to the task of compiling, updating, and making readily accessible a database of off-campus housing options. These options may include rooms for rent, corporate housing, and other furnished housing arrangements. Schools may also wish to refer admitted students to local home-stay placement providers for help in finding a suitable home-stay placement. The advantage of this arrangement is that the school's commitment of time and effort to coordinating these accommodations is minimal. Typically, it can involve little more than the referral itself, along with some quality-control monitoring and assessment of students' experiences in the home-stays.

Recruitment Strategies

Most of the recruitment strategies and activities discussed in this chapter apply to international student recruitment at the community college, so readers who haven't already read previous chapters are advised to do so. The following strategies are intended to supplement the material presented earlier.

Highlighting Advantages

Naturally it makes sense for schools to highlight many or all of the unique advantages of the U.S. community college when engaging in international student recruitment.

Low Tuition Costs

Highlight the fact that community college tuition prices are often lower than those at four-year schools. Draw attention to the low cost of your tuition in brochures, on your Web site, and in your e-mail communications and phone conversations with prospective students and their families.

University Transfer

Where applicable, community colleges looking to increase international student enrollments should highlight their four-year university transfer connections. Emphasize transfer agreements, such as transfer admission guarantees and other formalized transfer pathways. If your school has a transfer center, and/or holds university transfer-related workshops and events, share this information with prospective students and their families. If representatives from four-year schools regularly visit your campus, advertise this fact to students.

Small Classes and Focus on Learning

Because class sizes tend to be smaller at community colleges than at four-year public universities, international students are less likely to get lost in the crowd, particularly in metropolitan areas. The cozy atmosphere of a U.S. community college can make for an easier adjustment to life in America, especially for an international student grappling with acculturation issues. The institutional emphasis on learning—as opposed to learning plus research—can also be discussed with more discriminating students and their parents.

English Language Admission Policies

Colleges with ESL and/or intensive English programs benefit by factoring these offerings into their admission policies. International students without demonstrated English language ability can be "conditionally admitted" to your college. These students undertake full-time English language study until their English skills have improved enough to enable them to matriculate.

You may want to allow students alternative means of demonstrating English proficiency beside the TOEFL. The International English Language Testing System (IELTS) is the most popular alternative to the TOEFL. Some colleges also accept students' completion of a certain level of English studies at local intensive English language programs in lieu of a TOEFL or IELTS score.

Power of Partnerships

Community colleges need not go it alone in actively recruiting international students. Partnering with other institutions on joint or consortium-based efforts is a practical strategy likely to yield real results.

Partnering with Four-Year Universities

Four-year universities routinely receive inquiries from prospective international students who may not be admissible based upon their academic background, but who nonetheless may be admitted to a nearby community college. It would be helpful then to the student and the university if the student is referred to a specific contact person at a local area community college. At community colleges with strong relationships with four-year universities, students may be able to avail themselves of transfer admission guarantees or similar arrangements. In these instances students are reassured that they are not being denied admission by the university, instead they are provided with a clear, alternative pathway to gain admission as a transfer student a few years later.

Students whose academic backgrounds are strong enough to gain admission to the university of their choice may be unable to afford the higher tuition costs involved in university study. These students also benefit by being referred to a specific person at a nearby community college. The community college and university can work cooperatively to make such students aware of the potential cost savings of this route to university education.

Prominently feature your transfer university partners in your promotional materials. Highlight university transfer information on the international student section of your college's Web site. If taking part in overseas recruitment fairs, ensure that your booth is located next to or near those of partner universities, for the sake of convenient student referrals in each direction. Hold joint information sessions for prospective international students and their families. Schools can share the costs involved in undertaking these activities.

Invite university officials to conduct information sessions for current international students on your campus. This is a useful service that provides students looking to transfer a convenient means of interacting with sometimes difficult-to-reach university officials. It also assists the university interested in increasing international student enrollments.

Partnering with Local Area Intensive English Programs

Intensive English language programs can be rich sources of prospective international students for a community college that shares the same geographical area. While not all English language students are interested in pursuing degree program studies, many have their sights set on that eventual goal.

Your college can be featured in the partner language program's print-based and Web-based promotional media, and vice-versa. You can also co-locate near one another at overseas recruitment fairs, conduct joint seminars, and the like.

Many intensive English language programs welcome visits and hold regular transfer events on site for their students. Language program students frequently ask for information on higher education options in and around their local area. Therefore, you will want to have well-established referral channels for such inquiries.

An important advantage of this form of international student recruitment is that it takes place locally and the costs are minimal. Because they are already in the United States, ESL students are more likely to enroll at your school than are students applying from overseas. These "transfer students" already hold visas and typically require less assistance with various aspects of adjustment and acculturation than do newly arrived students. They are more likely to know how to use local transportation and/or have their own car to do the same, for example. They tend to require less assistance finding accommodations, as well.

Joining International Student Recruitment-Related Consortia

Depending upon your community college's geographical area, there may be consortia-based international student recruitment efforts. Examples of such state-based groups include the Education and Training Export Consortium (ETEC) in California; Destination Indiana; Study Illinois; Study Oregon; Study Wisconsin; Study Washington, and others. The American Association of Community Colleges boasts an array of international recruitment-related resources on its Web site, www.aacc.nche.edu/.

Involvement in consortium-led international student outreach and recruitment efforts affords you many advantages. These include the pooling of resources with other like-minded institutions in your local area and the sharing of knowledge and best practices among institutions. Many consortia do not charge membership fees. Where fees do exist, these are typically negligible.

Outreach to Parents

Most prospective community college students are still in high school, or have recently graduated, at the time they begin evaluating schools in the United States. Given their youth, these students often rely on their parents and other family members during the application and decisionmaking processes. Family influence is further amplified in certain cultures, so parents, siblings, and extended family members have a stronger impact on students' lives than is typically the case among American students.

Given these age and cultural considerations, it is important to ensure that your outreach and communications are focused toward both the student and the student's family. A student's parents—and to a lesser extent his or her siblings—will often care much more about the safety and security of your college campus, and the area in which it is located, than the student may. Parents may also be more interested in demonstrable examples of how their investment in their child's education is going to "pay off" in the form of their ability to transfer to high-quality U.S. universities.

Know Your Students

An often overlooked source of good information about how to best position your college in an increasingly crowded marketplace is your own international student body. Current international students are often eager and willing to share their opinions about how they came to choose your school. Students can be engaged and asked to provide insights into their decisionmaking process. These insights can in turn be used in the conduct of outreach and recruitment activity.

Various market research methodologies exist to help you gain such insights. Quantitative methods, like surveys, can be effective. Qualitative measures, like focus groups or one-on-one interviews, can also be useful. Regardless of the methodologies, market research of this kind must be approached with an open mind. Fixed, preconceived notions can bias the analysis of results. Also, care must be taken to ensure that student participants are representative of the countries you want to target.

Focus to Win-Win

Anecdotal and statistical evidence suggest that recent growth in international enrollments at U.S. community colleges is likely to continue. Therefore, college officials interested in beginning or intensifying outreach to international students will find this a promising time to do so. By focusing on what is unique about community colleges and partnering with others in the local area, recruiting international students can be a win-win situation—benefitting students and schools alike.

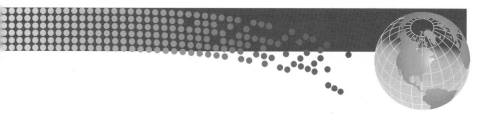

Graduate Programs

Steven L. Shaw

The importance of international graduate students in U.S. colleges and in the business world has to some extent been recognized for at least several decades. International graduate students are often the best and brightest from their home countries and contribute as students, teachers, and researchers. Recently this recognition has reached the front pages of even local newspapers as the importance of international graduate students is illustrated by the many benefits they contribute locally and nationally. Nearly 50 percent of the founding partners of Silicon Valley tech and engineering start-ups are foreign-born and educated in or immigrants to the United States. The U.S. Patent and Trademark Office has reported that the percentage of patents filed by foreigners living in the U.S. (and many of these educated in the U.S. as well) has tripled in just the last decade—an indication of both the quantity and quality of knowledge creation. Author Thomas Friedman is quoted as saying "I believe that our ability to cream off the first-round intellectual draft choices from around the world remains one of our great competitive advantages. We should pin a green card to any foreign student who comes here and gets a Ph.D." (*Time,* September 4, 2008, "10 questions for Thomas Friedman").

While the growth of total international student enrollment over the past 50 years is startlingly (with a nearly 15-fold increase from some 40,000 in 1956-57 to more than 580,000 in 2006-07), the shift in academic degree level often goes unnoticed. Since 1981-82, the percentage of those enrolled in bachelor's degree programs and those in graduate degree programs has reversed direction. In 1981-82, nearly 50 percent of international students were enrolled in bachelor's degree programs and 35 percent in graduate programs (including professional degree programs). But in 2006-07, it is almost the opposite: 29 percent are in bachelor's programs and more than 45 percent in graduate programs. In just 25 years international graduate enrollment has more than doubled from 115,000 to 264,000. In many universities they are the lifeblood of the STEM disciplines (Science, Technology, Engineering, and Mathematics) and provide essential teaching and research duties as teaching assistants (TAs) and research assistants (RAs).

Before examining the international graduate recruitment process, it will be helpful to review three factors that have greatly changed recruitment.

The Post-September 11 World

The most notable of these factors that has affected international student recruitment and enrollment is that of September 11, 2001, with the tightening of student visa policies and a number of new systems and procedures that were implemented. While these were intended to improve and increase national security, there were unintended consequences and a learning curve for the users of those systems and procedures.

In 2003 the Student and Exchange Visitor Information System (SEVIS) was launched, and U.S. colleges were required to issue certificates of visa eligibility (the I-20 Form for F-1 Student Visas and the DS-2019 Form for J-1 Exchange Visitor Visas) and to monitor enrolled students through the system. Students were required to pay a SEVIS fee of $100 as well as the visa application fee. Initially, there was confusion and delay as schools, students, and consulates became familiar with the new processes and systems.

With these hurdles and the general sense that they were not welcome in the United States, prospective students examined whether they needed to leave their home education system or if they should simply choose another host country. Doctoral students, and post-doc and research scholars in particular, faced an especially difficult time because of background security checks. If visa applicants intend to study in any of the 200-plus "majors" included in the Critical Fields List (CFL)/Technology Alert List (TAL), the consular officer is required to confirm that the student does not intend to use the knowledge for purposes that could potentially be used to harm the national security of the U.S. If there is any doubt (and if the student is from one of the designated State Sponsors of Terrorism), a Security Advisory Opinion (SAO) involving a background check must be conducted in Washington, DC. Fortunately, the SAO process has now been streamlined and most background checks do not take more than one or two months.

In the meantime, other host countries made much of the fact that they did not have such hurdles and welcomed the students through a much more streamlined process. U.S. colleges must be proactive and help students understand the extended timeline required to apply to U.S. graduate programs. And in the case of doctoral students, some institutions have found it useful and necessary to engage their graduate deans and chairs to intervene on behalf of students facing visa problems and background checks.

The Global Economy

The second factor affecting the recruitment of international students (and especially graduate students) is the global economy. International recruitment and enrollment is impacted by the global economy in much the same way that domestic student enrollment is affected by local economies. When the economy is strong and jobs are plentiful, many students defer formal education for a well-paying job; when the economy is weak, the markets are unstable, and the job market is tight, many students enroll in school with the hope that future rewards (a better job and higher salary) will be worth the present investment. Prospective international students react in much the same way it is just a much more complex scenario to analyze.

In general, when the economy of an international student's home country is strong, there has to be a very compelling reason to forego a steady job and salary to instead pursue an advanced degree in the United States. The most compelling incentive for most students would be a full scholarship so that there is little or no out-of-pocket investment on the part of the student. In flat economies and assuming that the student has some financial capability, many students are willing to pursue an advanced degree knowing that they are investing in a better future. A very weak or volatile economy has much the same influence as a very strong economy but for different reasons. When a national economy is so weak or unstable (as in the case of the 1997-98 Asian economic crisis or the collapse of Argentina's economy in 1999), many students prefer to wait it out not knowing if it is worth investing in an uncertain future. Either way, U.S. recruiters should be aware of the economic situation in other countries and make that part of their assessment in determining where and when to recruit.

The U.S. economy also affects international recruitment (especially graduate student recruitment) as it is related to the possibility of future employment in the United States. Although international students enter in a nonimmigrant visa class and without the intention of working or immigrating to the United States, the reality is that 1) there are legal pathways to postgraduation employment (through Optional Practical Training (OPT) and in some cases the H1B temporary worker visa program), and 2) that the availability and likelihood of such employment impacts recruitment and enrollment. For example, when the "dot com bust" of the 1990s occurred, there was an almost immediate decline in interest and enrollment of international students in the computer sciences. This was not necessarily because these types of jobs would be impacted in their home country, but rather because the possibility of OPT and an H1B job in that field in the United States were so unlikely.

In 2008, the United States created a 17-month OPT extension option for graduates of certain STEM disciplines, allowing such students to engage in a total of 29 months of OPT if they work for a U.S. employer registered in the E-Verify program. The interim rule was made final in 2009, allowing a 29-month program for STEM discipline graduates. While this change may increase interest and enrollment, the United States still lags far behind other countries (notably such as Australia, Canada, and the United Kingdom) in tying recruitment of international students to a skilled worker policy, and ultimately to an immigration policy. Again, U.S. recruiters must be aware of different training and employment policies and plan recruitment efforts accordingly.

The Bologna Process

The third major event impacting international graduate recruitment is the Bologna process. Named for the declaration signed at the University of Bologna (Italy) in 1999 by some 45 European signatory countries, the Bologna Process is to increase student mobility. To facilitate student mobility, signatory countries are moving toward a common higher education system with three cycles (bachelor's, master's, and doctoral) rather than the old, long first degrees that often took five or more years to complete. One major outcome of the Bologna Process is the three-year bachelor's degree. By 2010, most European first degrees will be the three-year bachelor's degrees (with the exception of some professional and engineering degrees).

U.S. higher education is still grappling with the Bologna Process and acceptance of three-year degrees. While some U.S. schools have stated that they will not accept the new degrees, the Council of Graduate Schools (CGS) reported in its 2006 CGS International Graduate Admissions Survey that 56 percent of polled schools said the three-year European bachelor's degrees were not an issue, that nearly 50 percent had adopted policies evaluating the three-year degree as equivalent to a U.S. bachelor's degree, and that another nearly 30 percent stated they did not reject the three-year degrees but evaluated each applicant on an individual basis (regardless of degree length).

Since only six percent of international graduate students come from Europe, one might think that the new three-year bachelor's degrees would have little impact on recruitment and enrollment of international students in the United States. But the Bologna Process reaches far beyond Europe because an increasing number of foreign students from traditional "sending" countries like China, India, and Korea are enrolling in undergraduate and graduate programs (often taught in English) in nontraditional host countries such as France, Germany, and The Netherlands. U.S. market share of international students has declined steadily since the 1970s, from a commanding 37 percent of the market to 22 percent in 2007.

Where to Recruit

A combination of factors such as visas and immigration-related policies, employment regulations, economic situations, competition from other countries, and higher education policies such as the Bologna Process all impact U.S. recruitment and enrollment of international graduate students. Thus it is important to conduct a region- or country-specific assessment of potential markets for your school's specific programs. What is a good market for one program may not be the case for another.

A simplified SWOT analysis (see Chapter 2.2: Creating a Strategic Plan for more information) focusing on "push-pull" factors is a relatively easy way to evaluate existing markets and to assess potential new markets. The factors should be as specific as possible to a school/program and to the country in question. For example, if one is considering recruiting engineering students from Japan, a much simplified push-pull table might look as follows.

What pulls them to school X in the United States (internal Strengths)	What pushes them from Japan (outside Opportunities)
Ranked in top 25 in the United States Top-notch laboratories World-class faculty Cutting-edge research Interaction with other students from around the world Opportunities for publishing and conference presentations Known for thinking "outside the box" Strong possibility for OPT in industry leader	Rigidity of education system Inability for independent research Homogeneous student population Lack of global interaction
What pushes them away from school X in the United States (internal Weakness)	**What pulls them to stay in Japan (external Threat)**
High cost English language proficiency Complex admission process	Adequate access to higher education Relatively low cost Alumni connections for employment

However, a similar push-pull table for Indian M.B.A. students in a weak U.S. economy might look very different.

What pulls them to school X in the United States	What pushes them from India
Ranked in top 25 in the United States World-class faculty Cutting-edge research Known for thinking "outside the box" and knowledge creation	Lack of access to higher education Too much rote-learning and exam-based system Inability for independent research Lack of global interaction
What pushes them away from school X in the United States	**What pulls them to stay in India**
High cost Few scholarships Weak economy might mean that OPT and potential for H1B are more difficult to obtain	Relatively low cost Strong economy means jobs are plentiful Wages are increasing Cost of living is much lower

With very basic research (including focus groups of currently enrolled students), the push-pull analysis is a quick and easy way to evaluate where to begin recruiting and whether to continue recruiting.

Three International Graduate Recruitment Models

A Centralized Approach to Recruitment

Enrollment management and graduate recruitment at U.S. universities runs the gamut from limited central coordination to complete decentralization of all responsibility to the departments. It is rare to find recruitment, application processing, and financial aid combined into a one-stop service center as is common in *undergraduate* enrollment centers. However, some schools do use a centralized approach for recruitment. In schools with this centralized model, responsibility for recruitment would generally be placed with the Graduate School. This single office would determine where, when, and how to market and recruit; in addition, this office would control the budget. In some cases the Graduate School may be involved in the follow-up communication, but more likely inquiry records would be turned over to the relevant academic programs for follow-up.

The advantage of a highly centralized approach is a unified and uniform approach to recruitment based on the objectives of the wider institution. Rather than a dozen different departments engaging in a dozen different recruitment activities, a single office may be more efficient and cost effective. However, this model requires highly trained staff who are familiar with all of the intricacies of many different programs.

Decentralized Graduate Recruitment

Much more likely is the decentralized model in which individual graduate programs are entirely responsible for their own marketing and recruitment. Faculty members are often the best recruiters because they know their programs and the needs of the department. Faculty often correspond with colleagues overseas, and with prospective students, well before the normal admission cycle begins. In competitive majors such as physics and chemistry, keeping abreast of the recruitment process is critical. Some faculty are very informed about the strong departments in their disciplines at foreign universities. With e-mail, faculty at U.S. universities can correspond easily with a prospective student's professors early in the process to get references. Because faculty typically play a significant role in the admission process at the graduate level, their role in making contacts with foreign colleagues and prospective students is crucial in the delicate process of attracting graduate students.

Inquiries from prospective graduate students arrive at the institution in a much different way than do undergraduate inquiries. Students may have learned about a university from their current professors or from a friend studying in the United States; from research papers, professional journals, alumni, or a search letter; or through Internet searches. International graduate students, like their domestic counterparts, are usually more focused in their educational goals than are undergraduates and wish to communicate directly with the faculty to discern mutual interest and to determine whether funding will be available. Individual faculty are concerned about filling their classes and not about feeding central database information. All of these factors make it more difficult to understand the graduate student applicant pool.

Competition for the best students is intense, and negotiations for high-quality international graduate students may begin well before the expected year of enrollment. Where major funding is at stake, program deadlines fall in January so that students can be considered for teaching and research assistantships. While it is true that admission offers go out during spring and even into late summer, institutions that want to compete for the highest-quality students must recruit actively during the fall semester, or earlier, and make offers of graduate assistantships as early as February.

Because recruitment activities for graduate students are specific to the individual disciplines, many of the functions normally performed by a central admission or enrollment service at the undergraduate level are performed at the *department* level for graduate students. Department staff may do mailings, collect and process applications, send preliminary admission and financial aid offers, and so on. Departments are not always allotted resources to handle such tasks, however. Institutions should consider the advantages of centralizing some of the services for graduate student admission to increase efficiency, reduce costs, and improve services. Faculty must still play an important role in the contact with prospective students, but asking them to mail and then process applications are not good uses of their time.

A Mixed Model

A third model for international graduate recruitment is a mixed model and this, in fact, is probably the most common. In a mixed model there is some sharing of responsibility for planning, budgeting, and implementing a recruitment plan between an office that is somewhat centralized but actively involves the individual graduate programs. In some institutions this may be an office of international education (overseeing all aspects of international programs and functions) or an office of international student/scholar services (primarily responsible for SEVIS reporting, student orientation, and student services). Regardless of the specific office, the structure is typically one where the recruiters represent the entire university (graduate and undergraduate regardless of discipline), but follow-up and processing will be turned over to the individual departments.

Like the centralized recruitment model, this mixed model requires well-trained and very knowledgeable staff who are able to speak to all programs and all requirements. This mixed model works best if the recruiters are full-time recruiters involved only in enrollment management, marketing, recruiting, and follow-up.

A unique mixed model approach has been designed by Purdue University. In the Purdue model, the office of International Students and Scholars (ISS) is the central office responsible for all general (undergraduate and graduate) recruitment. In an effort to involve specific graduate programs in recruitment, ISS launched a grant competition process whereby graduate departments submit a grant proposal for a specific overseas recruitment event. In a very competitive process, ISS then selects and funds one to three graduate programs to conduct the overseas recruitment event (for example, attending college/career fairs). Selected programs typically do much more than just attend a public college fair; they often build in visits to key universities (to specific departments), host alumni events, develop new exchange programs, and have time set aside for student interviews (often key in determining scholarship recipients and assistantships). This unique model still leaves the budget and broad enrollment management planning responsibilities within the central office, but offers a powerful way to involve graduate departments.

Regardless of the general recruitment model (highly centralized, highly decentralized, or some version of a mixed model), it is imperative that an international graduate student recruitment program be carefully designed, proactive, and balanced. Recognize that it may take several years to build a successful program and show results (typically, at least three years is needed to see measurable results).

Activities and Tips for Success

- Develop an advisory board or committee of faculty in the disciplines selected for focus. Involve faculty at every stage of planning, and enlist their active support in implementing strategies. The committee should include some personnel from related disciplines, some of whom have experience in recruiting internationally. It should also include foreign-born faculty who can advise the committee of appropriate means of contact in the selected countries.

- Use the Graduate Record Examination (GRE) Search Service to buy prospective student names by discipline. Requests for names can be sorted by the self-reported information given at the time of test registration and the test results, much like the SAT Student Search Service for undergraduates. The GRE Search Service bulletin lists helpful statistics about past student volumes, intended majors, preferred study location, and degree objective to help make decisions on search criteria or whether the search service will be useful to your institution. Information on cost for participation in the GRE Search Service is available on GRE's Web site (www.ets.org/gre/search.html).

- Be sure the university Web site has complete information about academic programs and research projects for international students. Link departmental Web pages to the international student services office Web site so students can obtain answers about visas, arrival information, orientation, hosts, housing, other students from their country, and so on.

- Consider advertising in professional journals. This method is effective because it often reaches the people who are most likely to be interested in further study. Journal readers are serious professionals and opinion makers.

- Attend education fairs that will assist your institution in meeting its international graduate student goals. At university fairs, those representing graduate departments must have a thorough knowledge of highly sophisticated curricula, research areas, admission criteria, and possible financial support for all departments. Representatives should carry a directory showing faculty specialties, addresses, telephone and fax numbers, and e-mail addresses. Where feasible, the presence of a faculty member from the most targeted field(s) can increase the event's effectiveness. Because many fairs have general sessions on topics of broad interest to attendees, the faculty member might volunteer to do a presentation, thereby giving the institution a public relations advantage.

- When traveling, make appointments with department chairs at local universities, established placement agencies, and government officials who might potentially sponsor students (ministers of science and technology, human resources, finance, transportation, education, and so on). These contacts will take on greater significance as potential graduate students turn to faculty and counseling centers for advice about pursuing further education in the United States. It is also useful to visit with the staff at the local Fulbright commission and the EducationUSA office.

- Survey faculty to find out who is planning to travel abroad to attend conferences, conduct research, or even to take vacation. They may be able and willing to make contacts on behalf of the university in countries not specifically targeted and for minimal additional cost.

- Make overseas alumni, U.S. alumni living abroad as well as international alumni, an integral part of the program (see Chapter 4.2: Making the Most of Alumni Contacts). Be sure international alumni records are kept up to date. Keep former students informed of the developments in university academic programs. Former students are your best recruiters.

The recruitment of international graduate students should be a planned and well-managed activity—it is a question of whether the institution is managing the population or the population is managing the institution. Lack of management can result in skewed populations and lack of assurance that the best students are being recruited. As with the undergraduate population, knowledge of the market is important and personal attention to students will result in the most successful program.

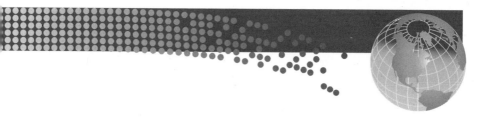

M.B.A. Programs

Liz Reisberg

Recruiting for master of business administration (M.B.A.) programs is different from other recruitment efforts. On the surface it might appear easier; anyone who has stood at an international university fair for at least an hour will confirm that a high percentage of the attendees seem to want M.B.A. degrees. Despite the apparent enthusiasm of fair attendees, recruiting appropriate candidates for M.B.A. programs is more challenging than one might expect.

The M.B.A. on the Educational Landscape

From an educational point of view, the M.B.A. is an anomaly. Every country has its own educational system and tradition. Even national systems that have evolved from British or French models have developed indigenous characteristics that make them unique. Yet the M.B.A. seems to be an international commodity whose shape depends less on the educational tradition of the host country and more on the influence of other M.B.A. programs. As a result, M.B.A. programs worldwide share similar curricula, reading lists, and pedagogies (such as the case method and team projects).

Remarkably, the M.B.A. curriculum is often taught in English, even at universities where all other programs are taught in another language. Some universities will offer two M.B.A. programs—one in the native language and another in English.

The other intriguing characteristic of M.B.A. programs is that they often exist apart from a university. In the United States, schools such as Thunderbird School of Global Management offer only graduate study in management; there are no undergraduate programs, no other graduate programs beyond the study of management-related fields, and no doctoral programs. Many of the new M.B.A. schools that have opened abroad have followed this model. Prestigious schools such as INSEAD, an international business school in France; International Institute for Management Development (IMD) in Switzerland; Instituto de Estudios Superiores en Administracion (IESA) in Venezuela; and Instituto Centroamericana de Administracion de Empresas (INCAE) in Costa Rica, are freestanding graduate business schools.

The United States was once the destination of choice for nearly all M.B.A. candidates going abroad—the U.S. economy was the largest and strongest in the world, so obviously it was assumed to be the place to learn about business and management. With so many new important economic centers emerging around the globe, internationally mobile candidates are now considering M.B.A. programs in other regions. While international enrollment in the United States has leveled off, the number of international students in Europe and Australia has grown rapidly.

Challenges to Recruiting for M.B.A. Programs

The M.B.A. was introduced in the United States. It was not considered a particularly prestigious or necessary degree until the early 1990's, when it suddenly became a hot commodity worldwide. At that time, M.B.A. programs were concentrated in the United States; thus, they became a powerful draw for international students anxious to take their place in an increasingly global economy. By obtaining an M.B.A. degree in the United States, young people demonstrated implicitly their capacity to succeed in another culture and their mastery of English. The return on investment of time and money was quite high, evidenced by the positions open to them in the international corporations that seemed to be opening offices everywhere. Many of those corporations were based in the United States and recruited heavily from U.S. business schools.

Not surprisingly, it didn't take long for new local M.B.A. programs to appear. The proliferation of international M.B.A. programs worldwide now makes it quite challenging for U.S. schools to claim distinguishing characteristics that would provide an obvious competitive edge. In other words, a Thai student who wants to earn an M.B.A., learn how to work and live in another culture in the process, and master English can enroll in a comparable program in Rotterdam, Barcelona, London, Melbourne, Fontainebleau, or Chicago. The M.B.A. is often offered in English regardless of the institution's location; it may be the first degree that truly reflects a global educational community.

One enormous challenge for M.B.A. programs is the extent to which international students rely on rankings. If you work at a top-ranked school, recruiting overseas is easier. While few educators are comfortable with the efficacy of rankings as a means to distinguish one academic program from another, rankings have a powerful influence on prospective students and (equally unfortunate) on prospective employers. International M.B.A. candidates are looking for schools with cachet that they can leverage for better employment opportunities upon graduation. It is a brave student who will choose to attend a program abroad that is unknown to others in his or her home country.

The university's reputation is often as influential as the ranking of the M.B.A. program. M.B.A. admission officers often market their M.B.A. separately from the university, relying on the "brand" of the business school. This is rarely advisable as names like Stern, Darden, Fuqua, and Olin rarely enjoy the same worldwide recognition as the name of the host university. When the university is well known in a country, then its M.B.A. program will be more attractive. If a university has many alumni (regardless of their degree program) in a particular country, that country is likely to be a strong market for the M.B.A. program.

The other implication of the linked prestige of the university is that prospective students expect all representatives of a university to have broad and deep knowledge about that university as a whole. Representatives who expect to have any credibility in the international M.B.A. market are well-advised to learn as much as possible about their university (for example, support services for international students, other graduate programs that might enroll the M.B.A. candidate's wife or husband, numbers of undergraduates from different countries, and so on). It is important to link the M.B.A. program to the larger university.

If your school is not at the top of the rankings, you must distinguish it from others, emphasizing the unique opportunities of your programs. Characteristics that attract attention might be the length of the program, dual-degree opportunities or unique specializations (such as business and law, hospital administration, or hotel administration), international focus, corporate consulting projects, geographic location, or cost. These competitive advantages should be highlighted in your literature, in your communication with prospective candidates, and in communications with those who help promote your programs. Simply stating that your business school has world-class faculty, international enrollment, and state-of-the-art facilities will not distinguish your program from others!

There are several logical sources of local support for your recruitment efforts, one of which—alumni—may sometimes have more local credibility than the rankings. The other sources are overseas educational advising centers (see Chapters 4.2: Making the Most of Alumni Contacts, and 4.3: Developing Overseas Relationships), M.B.A. admission consultants, test preparation centers, and local universities. More about each of these follows.

The Volatility in the Market

In an ideal world, it would be possible to recruit a balanced and diverse mix of international students to each incoming class but that is rarely the case. Too many unpredictable and/or uncontrollable factors shape the market.

Countries with strong currencies and rapidly growing economies are the most likely source of international M.B.A. students. In 2008, for example, that meant that the students most likely to pursue an M.B.A. abroad were in China and India where international companies were expanding activities rapidly, a circumstance that promised a good return for individuals investing time and resources in international M.B.A. programs abroad.

Countries with weaker economies (such as countries in Latin America and Africa in 2008) offer less promise as the cost of purchasing currency for education abroad is very high and the ROI (return on investment) is very low because employment opportunities will most likely be with local companies at modest salaries.

As mentioned above, the destination of choice is increasingly difficult to predict. Although the United States remains the most popular destination for prospective M.B.A. candidates, Europe and Australia are becoming strong competitors. The United Kingdom and Australia have employed aggressive strategies to encourage international students to enroll there. Australia claims to offer exposure to Asian economies, while the United Kingdom offers exposure to the European Union; these are attractive advantages to international M.B.A. students.

Keep in mind that many Asian countries aspire to be "destination" countries as well as "sending" countries, so it will not be surprising to see greater competition from China, India, Korea, and Japan for international students.

Finding Your Market

Although university M.B.A. fairs are very popular, it isn't always easy to find candidates there who are appropriate for your program.

M.B.A. admission officers often overlook their most obvious and promising markets—international graduates of undergraduate programs at their university and the friends of alumni. M.B.A. programs enroll individuals from a broad range of professional fields. The management skills taught in M.B.A. programs are important to engineers, accountants, journalists, lawyers, and specialists in international affairs, as well as to graduates of the undergraduate program in business. Several years after earning an undergraduate degree, many alumni find themselves moving into more senior positions within their organizations and are often ready for graduate study. These are people who are already familiar with the campus and its environs, have established relationships with people at the university that they continue to value, and are the most inclined to appreciate the value of a degree earned abroad.

Alumni and their friends are a very logical place to begin any recruitment strategy. Recent alumni are likely to have friends and colleagues who are considering graduate education abroad. The challenge is finding ways to communicate with this group and to integrate them into your recruitment strategy. Coordinate activities with the alumni office and undergraduate admission office so multiple departments do not badger alumni. (See Chapter 4.2: Making the Most of Alumni Contacts.)

For traveling admission officers who recruit undergraduate students overseas, a visit to the international and American high schools is the logical way to target the bulk of the U.S.-bound market. For most *graduate* programs, students enter immediately upon completing their undergraduate program, so a visit to the appropriate department at a foreign university would reach that market. But most M.B.A. schools want to enroll individuals with at least two years of work experience. That means that the best candidates are scattered among hundreds of employers in any given city at any given time. Although some employers encourage young managers to pursue an M.B.A. and, in some cases, even sponsor them, others would not welcome the news that an employee was planning to leave. As a result, employers are not always useful contacts on a recruitment trip.

Prospective M.B.A. students inevitably find their way to the EducationUSA office where they will register and/or take the Graduate Management Admissions Test (GMAT) and the TOEFL. It is wise to make certain that EducationUSA offices have information about your programs, and even wiser to establish a relationship with the individual advisers in the center. These professionals are an important link between your program and the local market. Like your alumni, educational advisers have the credibility to help candidates look beyond the rankings and consider programs that offer appropriate opportunities for their individual needs. Nearly all overseas advisers have e-mail addresses, and many attend the NAFSA Annual Conference where they welcome the chance to meet admission representatives and increase their knowledge of individual programs. For university representatives who travel alone internationally, the EducationUSA offices are an important stop.

In many cities there are M.B.A. admission consultants who guide individuals through the process of choosing an appropriate business school and then preparing a strong application. Since few students have experience with M.B.A. admission requirements (admission essays, letters of recommendation, interviews), this service can be extremely helpful. The quality of this service (as well as the quality of the consultant) varies a great deal though—some consultants operate with the highest professional and ethical standards, others do not.

Admission consultants can be excellent contacts who can support recruiting activities and provide valuable information about the local market, but admission officers are well-advised to do some research before deciding whom to contact.

There has also been an explosion of private centers that provide orientation to the admission tests. Some of these centers also offer advising. Admission officers should make every effort to learn as much as possible about how these centers operate, the qualifications of their staff, the promises they make to their clients, their fees, and their record of success. Sometimes the local educational advising center or alumni can help. A good relationship with a good test-prep center is a great way to promote and develop visibility for your school; on the other hand, a relationship with an unethical or incompetent center can do irreparable harm (see Chapter 4.4: Working with Third-Party Agents).

Collaboration with a local university often provides multiple advantages. The benefits generally come in the long term. Student exchanges, faculty exchanges, and joint case writing all help to enhance the local visibility and attractiveness of your school abroad and provide tremendous educational advantages back on your home campus.

Tours and Fairs

Several organizations offer events and activities overseas for recruitment. Some organizations specialize in M.B.A. fairs. Signing up for a fair or tour overseas may be the easiest way to jump into the international market, but not necessarily the most productive. Fairs generally draw from several hundred to several thousand students and provide a forum that will give your program much public exposure.

Keep in mind that for a school that has very little history in a country, participation in the fair alone may not be sufficient to produce a dramatic shift in international enrollment. If you do not represent a high-profile business school, it is possible to spend hours at a fair and not speak with any of the hundreds of attendees. Fairs require preparation and a strategy for engaging people who are meandering through the hall.

If your M.B.A. program or an undergraduate program has education abroad students in the city where you are attending a fair, invite them to join you. Prospective candidates are sometimes more comfortable approaching students than administrators. They (even non-M.B.A. students) can speak about the culture of the university, the benefits of the location, and student life with great credibility.

Participation in fairs is most successful when combined with other activities (such as those above) to build awareness of your M.B.A. program. It is most important to have a long-term strategy for building visibility, credibility, and prestige, something that generally requires time and persistence.

Following up with students you meet during travel is critical. Too many representatives pass contact information on to other staff members in their office; there may be no follow up at all or it may be impersonal. Most cultures value relationships very highly and personal follow-up can have a big impact!

Do Your Homework

The most successful recruiting begins with knowledge. Although trends do not necessarily define possibilities for your M.B.A. program, it is important to know what is going on. IIE (Institute of International Education) produces two important reports, *Open Doors* (http://opendoors.iienetwork.org/) and *Project Atlas* (www.atlas.iienetwork.org), that provide invaluable data about the international market as a whole. Graduate Management Admissions Council (GMAC) publishes trend data specifically about the M.B.A. market on their Web site (www.gmac.com/gmac). The Center for International Higher Education at Boston College (www.bc.edu/cihe) publishes these reports at their Web site, as well as other information about trends. Armed with this information, you'll be ready to promote your M.B.A. program to prospective applicants.

Appendixes

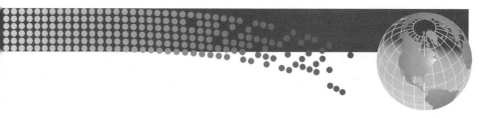

Publications and Internet Resources

Print Resources

2006 CGS International Graduate Admissions Survey. 2006
www.cgsnet.org

Multi-year examination of international graduate application, admission, and enrollment trends.

Brief Guide to U.S. Higher Education. 2001
www.acenet.edu/bookstore

Directory of Overseas Educational Advising Centers 2006
www.collegeboard.com

Detailed contact information for more than 470 centers in 160+ countries, includes international and APO/pouch addresses, e-mail, Web sites, and telephone and fax numbers.

Encyclopedia of Higher Education. 1992
Clark, B. R. and G. Neave, Pergamon Press. Review of higher education worldwide.

Immigration Classifications and Legal Employment of Foreign Nationals in the United States. 2008
NAFSA: Association of International Educators
www.nafsa.org

This essential poster, describing each immigrant and nonimmigrant classification, provides explicit information on employment eligibility and study options of visa holders in that category; updated to reflect statutory and regulatory changes effective as of February 2008.

The International Student Handbook
www.collegeboard.com

Published annually, directory of undergraduate and graduate study at U.S. colleges and universities compiled expressly for foreign students. Explains what colleges require of foreign students, how to apply, financial aid policies, and how to assess offerings.

NAFSA Adviser's Manual Online
NAFSA: Association of International Educators
www.nafsa.org/manual

> Since 1966, an indispensable reference containing detailed descriptions and analyses of current federal regulations affecting foreign students and scholars in the United States. Now online.

U.S. Tax Guide for Aliens (IRS publication 519) and U.S. Tax Treaties (IRS publication 901).
U.S. Internal Revenue Service. Free.
Download online from www.irs.ustreas.gov/formspubs/index.html

Internet Sites—U.S. Higher Education and Individual Educational Institutions

American School Counselor Association
www.schoolcounselor.org

> Provides links to a wide range of information about higher education institutions in the United States, including universities, community colleges, and business, technical, and trade schools.

Center for International Higher Education at Boston College
www.bc.edu/cihe

> Publishes on their Web site various reports as well as other information about trends.

The College Board
www.collegeboard.com

> Contains a college search feature that sorts for several variables, including type of school, majors, admissions, location, sports, and financial aid.

EduPASS
www.edupass.org.

> Direct and informative site, created specifically for international students, devoted to securing financing for higher education in the United States. A must-see for any international student considering study in the United States.

European Council of International Schools (ECIS)
www.ecis.org

Global Education Database
http://qesdb.cdie.org/ged/index.html

> An interactive program for accessing education data compiled from UNESCO sources. Statistics on international education and related developing-country socioeconomic conditions from 1970 to present, in easy-to-use electronic format.

Graduate Management Admissions Council (GMAC)
www.gmac.com/gmac

Publishes trend data specifically about the MBA market on their Web site.

Institute of International Education, IIE Network Linkages Portal
www.iienetwork.org/?p=Linkages

Links to articles and papers examining all aspects of international cooperation and global partnership, as well as links to other resources.

NAFSA: Association of International Educators
www.nafsa.org

NAFSA Recruitment, Admissions, and Preparation Knowledge Community
www.nafsa.org/RAP

Overseas Association of College Admission Counseling (OACAC)
www.oacac.com

U.S. Commercial Service
http://trade.gov/cs/

U.S. Department of State Bureau of Educational and Cultural Affairs
http://educationusa.state.gov/

Internet Sites—Cyber Recruitment Resources

European Foundation for Management Development
www.efmd.org/

Worldwide Internet Connectivity and Online Language Usage
www.internetworldstats.com/stats.htm

Mobile Advertising
Chetan Sharma, Joe Herzog, and Victor Melfi

www.chetansharma.com/Mobile%20Advertising%20Full%20TOC.pdf

Search Engine Pay-Per-Click Campaigns
Targeting by language and geography

https://adwords.google.com/

http://searchmarketing.yahoo.com/

www.naver.com/ (in South Korea)

www.baidu.com/ (in China)

Mobile Marketing Vendors

www.admob.com/

www.mkhoj.com/

Bulk SMS (text messaging) Vendor

www.clickatell.com/

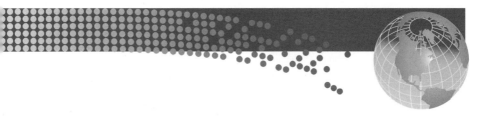

Ministries of Education by Country

Albania	Ministry of Education and Science	www.mash.gov.al/
Algeria	1. Ministère de l'Èducation Nationale (Ministry of National Education)	www.meducation.edu.dz
	2. Ministère de l'Enseignement supérieur et de la recherché scientifique (Ministry of Higher Education and Scientific Research)	www.mesrs.edu.dz/
Argentina	1. Ministerio de Educación, Ciencia, y Tecnología (Ministry of Education, Science, and Technology)	www.mcye.gov.ar
	2. Comisión Nacional de Evaluación y Acreditación Universitaria (National Commission of University Evaluation and Accreditation)	www.coneau.edu.ar/
Armenia	Ministry of Education and Science	www.edu.am/
Australia	Department of Education, Science, and Training	www.dest.gov.au/
Austria	Bundesministerium für Bildung, Wissenschaft, und Kultur (Federal Ministry of Education, Science, and Culture)	www.bmbwk.gv.at/ fremdsprachig/index.xml
Azerbaijan	Ministry of Education	http://edu.gov.az/
Bahamas	Ministry of Education and Department of Education	http://webserv. bahamaseducation.com/
Bahrain	Ministry of Education	www.education.gov.bh/
Bangladesh	Ministry of Education	http://dns3.bdcom.com/ iactive/moe/index.html

(Continued)

Barbados	Ministry of Education, Youth Affairs, and Culture	www.edutech2000.gov.bb/
Belarus	Ministry of Education	www.minedu.unibel.by/
Belgium	Communauté Flamande Administration of Higher Education and Scientific Research, Ministry of the Flemish Community	www.ond.vlaanderen.be/
	(Communauté Française) Direction générale de l'Enseignement non obligatoire et de la Recherche scientifique, Ministère de la Communauté française	www.cfwb.be/infosup/
Belize	Ministry of Education and Sports	www.belize.gov.bz/cabinet/ c_hyde/welcome.shtml
Bolivia	Ministerio de Educación (Ministry of Education)	www.minedu.gov.bo/
Brazil	Ministério de Eduçacão e Desport (Ministry of Education and Sports)	www.mec.gov.br/
Brunei	Ministry of Education	www.brunet.bn/gov/moe/ about.htm
Bulgaria	Ministry of Education and Science	www.minedu.government.bg/
Cambodia	Ministry of Education, Youth, and Sport	www.moeys.gov.kh/
Cameroon	Ministère de l'Enseignement Supérieur (Ministry of Higher Education)	www.minesup.gov.cm/
Canada (Each province has its own agency)	*Alberta* Alberta Learning	www.learning.gov.ab.ca/
	British Columbia Ministry of Advanced Education, Training, and Technology	www.aett.gov.bc.ca/
	Ministry of Education	www.bced.gov.bc.ca/
	Manitoba Education and Training	www.edu.gov.mb.ca/
	New Brunswick Department of Education	www.gnb.ca/0000/
	Newfoundland Department of Education and Training	www.gov.nf.ca/edu/
	Northwest Territories Department of Education, Culture and Employment	http://siksik.learnnet.nt.ca/
	Nova Scotia Nova Scotia Department of Education	www.ednet.ns.ca/

(Continued)

Canada (continued)	*Nunavut* Department of Education	www.gov.nu.ca/education/eng/
	Ontario Ministry of Education	www.edu.gov.on.ca/
	Prince Edward Island Department of Education	www.gov.pe.ca/educ/
	Québec Ministère de l'Éducation (Ministry of Education)	www.meq.gouv.qc.ca/
	Saskatchewan Saskatchewan Department of Education	www.sasked.gov.sk.ca/
	Yukon Department of Education	www.education.gov.yk.ca/
Chile	1. Ministerio de Educación (Ministry of Education)	www.mineduc.cl/
	2. Consejo Superior de Educación (Council on Higher Education)	www.cse.cl/
China	Ministry of Education	www.moe.edu.cn/
Colombia	Instituto Colombiano para el Formento de la Educación Superior (Colombian Institute for the Formation of Higher Education)	www.icfes.gov.co/
Costa Rica	Ministerio de de Educación Pública (Ministry of Public Education)	www.mep.go.cr/
Côte d'Ivoire	Ministry of National Education and Basic Education	www.refer.ci/ivoir_ct/edu/accueil.htm
Croatia	Ministry of Science and Technology	www.mzos.hr/default.asp
Cuba	Ministerio de Educación (Ministry of Education)	www.rimed.cu/
Cyprus	Ministry of Education and Culture	www.moec.gov.cy/
Czech Republic	Ministerstvo školství, mládeže, a telovýchovy (Ministry of Education, Youth, and Sports)	www.msmt.cz/
Denmark	Undervisningsministeriet (Ministry of Education)	www.uvm.dk/
Djibouti	Ministère de l'Èducation Nationale et de l'Enseignement Supérieur (Ministry of National Education and Higher Education)	www.education.gov.dj/

(Continued)

Dominican Republic	1. Secretaría de Estado de Educación y Cultura (State Department of Education and Culture)	www.see.gov.do/sitesee.net/default.aspx
	2. Secretaría de Estado de Educación Superior, Ciencia y Tecnología (State Department of Higher Education, Science and Technology)	www.seescyt.gov.do/
Ecuador	1. Ministerio de Educación y Culturas (Ministry of Education and Cultures)	www.mec.gov.ec/
	2. Consejo Nacional de Educación Superior (National Council of Higher Education)	www.conesup.net/
Egypt	Ministry of Education	www.emoe.org
El Salvador	Ministerio de Educación	www.mined.gob.sv/
Estonia	Vabaiigi Haridusminsteerium (Ministry of Education)	www.hm.ee/
Finland	Opetusministeriö (Ministry of Education)	www.minedu.fi/
France	Ministère de l'Education nationale (Ministry of National Education)	www.education.gouv.fr/index.php
Germany	Federal Ministry of Education and Research (Bundesministerium für Bildung und Forschung)	www.bmbf.de/
Ghana	Ministry of Education	www.ghana.edu.gh/
Greece	Ministry of National Education and Religious Affairs	www.ypepth.gr/en_ec_home.htm
Guatemala	Ministerio de Educación	www.mineduc.gob.gt/
Guyana	Ministry of Education	www.sdnp.org.gy/minedu/
Hong Kong	Education and Manpower Bureau	www.emb.gov.hk/
Hungary	Ministry of Education	www.om.hu/
Iceland	Ministry of Education, Science, and Culture	http://brunnur.stjr.is/interpro/mrn/mrn-eng.nsf/pages/frontpage
India	1. Department of Education	www.education.nic.in/
	2. All India Council for Technical Education	www.aicte.ernet.in/
Indonesia	Ministry of Education and Culture	www.pdk.go.id/
Iran	Ministry of Science, Research, and Technology	www.mche.or.ir/
Iraq	Ministry of Education	www.moeiraq.info/
Ireland	1. Department of Education and Science	www.education.ie
	2. Higher Education Authority	www.hea.ie/

(Continued)

Israel	Ministry of Education, Culture, and Sports	www.education.gov.il/
Italy	Ministry for Universities and Scientific and Technological Research (Ministerio dell'Università e della Ricerca Scientifica e Tecnologica)	www.murst.it/
Jamaica	Ministry of Education, Youth, and Culture	www.moec.gov.jm/
Japan	Ministry of Education, Culture, Sports, Science, and Technology	www.mext.go.jp/english/
Jordan	Ministry of Education	www.moe.gov.jo/
	Ministry of Higher Education	www.moe.gov.jo/
Kenya	Ministry of Education, Science, and Technology	www.education.go.ke/
Kuwait	1. Ministry of Education	www.moe.edu.kw/
	2. Ministry of Higher Education	www.mohe.edu.kw/
	3. Public Authority for Applied Education and Training	www.paaet.edu.kw/
Latvia	Ministry of Education and Science (Izglitibas un Zinatnes Ministrija)	www.izm.lv/
Lebanon	Ministère de l'Èducation et de l'Enseignement Supérieur	www.crdp.org/
Lithuania	Ministry of Education and Science	www.smm.lt/
Luxembourg	Ministère de l'Èducation Nationale, de la formation professionnalle, et des sports	www.men.lu/
Macau	Department of Education and Youth Affairs	www.mext.go.jp/english/
(TFYR) of Macedonia	Ministry of Education and Science	www.mofk.gov.mk/
Madagascar	Ministère de l'Enseignement Supérieur	www.refer.mg/madag_ct/edu/minesup/
Malaysia	Ministry of Education	www.moe.gov.my/findex.htm
Maldives	Ministry of Education	www.moe.gov.mv/
Mauritania	Institut Pédagogique Nationale	www.mr.refer.org/ipn/
Mauritius	Ministry of Education and Scientific Research	http://ncb.intnet.mu/education/
Mexico	1. Secretaría de Educación Pública	www.sep.gob.mx/
	2. Associación Nacional de Universdidades y Instituciones de Educación Superior	www.anuies.mx/
Moldova	Ministerul Educatiei (Ministry of Education)	www.edu.md/
Monaco	Direction de l'Èducation Nationale, de la jeunesse, et des sports	www.education.gouv.mc/

(Continued)

Mongolia	Mongolian National Council for Higher Education Accreditation	www.accmon.mn/english/1_2.htm
Morocco		www.men.gov.ma/ www.dfc.gov.ma/
Mozambique	Ministry of Higher Education, Science, and Technology	www.mesct.gov.mz/
Namibia	Ministry of Education and National Institute for Educational Development	www.nied.edu.na/
Nepal	Ministry of Education and Sports	www.moe.gov.np/ministry/index.php
	Department of University Education, Ministry of Education, Culture, and Science (Ministerie van Onderwijs, Cultuur, en Wetenschappen)	www.minocw.nl
New Zealand	Ministry of Education	www.minedu.govt.nz/
Nicaragua		www.mecd.gob.ni/ www.cnu.edu.ni/
Norway		www.dep.no/ufd/ www.uhr.no/
Oman		www.moe.gov.om/moe/ www.mohe.gov.om/
Pakistan		www.moe.gov.pk/ www.hec.gov.pk
Palestinian Authority	Ministry of Education	www.moe.gov.ps/
Panama	Ministerio de Educación	www.meduc.gob.pa/
Paraguay	Ministerio de Educación y Cultura	www.mec.gov.py/
Peru	Ministerio de Educación	www.minedu.gob.pe/
Philippines		www.deped.gov.ph/ www.tesda.gov.ph/ www.ched.gov.ph/
Poland	Ministry of National Education	www.men.waw.pl/
Portugal		www.min-edu.pt/ www.mces.pt/
Qatar	Ministry of Education	www.moe.edu.qa/Arabic/

(Continued)

Romania	Ministry of Education, Research, and Youth	www.edu.ro/
Russian Federation		www.ed.gov.ru/ www.nica.ru/main.en.phtml
St. Lucia	Ministry of Education, Human Resource Development, Youth, and Sports	www.education.gov.lc/
Saudi Arabia		www.moe.gov.sa/ www.mohe.gov.sa/ www.gotevot.edu.sa/ www.girlsedu.gov.sa/
Senegal	Ministère de l'Éducation	www.education.gouv.sn/
Serbia and Montenegro		www.gom.cg.yu/eng/minprosv/ www.gom.cg.yu/eng/minprosv/
Singapore	Ministry of Education	www.moe.gov.sg/
Slovak Republic	Ministry of Education of the Slovak Republic (Ministerstvo_kolstva SR)	www.education.gov.sk/
Slovenia	Ministry of Education, Science, and Sports	www.mszs.si/slo/
South Africa		http://education.pwv.gov.za/ www.saqa.org.za/
South Korea	Ministry of Education and Human Resources Development	www.moe.go.kr/
Spain	Division of Universities, Ministry of Education, Culture, and Sports (Dirección general de Universidades, Ministerio de Educación, Cultura, y Deporte)	www.mec.es/
Sri Lanka	Department of Examinations	www.doenets.lk/
	University Grants Commission	www.ugc.ac.lk/
Sudan	Ministry of Education	www.moe-sd.com/index1.htm (in Arabic)
Swaziland	Ministry of Education	www.gov.sz/home.asp?pid=57
Sweden		www.regeringen.se/ www.hsv.se/

(Continued)

Switzerland	1. Federal Office for Education and Science	www.bbw.admin.ch/
	2. Swiss Conference of Cantonal Ministers of Public Education	www.bbw.admin.ch/
	3. Swiss University Conference	www.cus.ch/
Taiwan ROC	Ministry of Education	english.moe.gov.tw
Tanzania	Government, Education	www.tanzania.go.tz/ educationf.html
Thailand	Ministry of Education	www.moe.go.th/
Trinidad and Tobago	Ministry of Science, Technology, and Tertiary Education	www.stte.gov.tt/
Tunisia	Ministè de l'Enseignement Supérieur	www.mes.tn/
Turkey	1. Ministry of National Education (Milli Eötim Bakanlyoy)	www.meb.gov.tr/
	2. Council on Higher Education	www.yok.gov.tr/
Uganda	Ministry of Education and Sports	www.education.go.ug/
Ukraine	Ministry of Education and Science	http://education.gov.ua/pls/edu/ educ.home.ukr
United Arab Emirates	Ministry of Education and Youth	www.education.gov.ae/
	Ministry of Higher Education and Scientific Research	www.uae.gov.ae/mohe/
United Kindgom	Department for Education and Skills	www.dfes.gov.uk
	1. Qualifications and Curriculum Authority	www.qca.org.uk/
	2. Qualifications, Curriculum and Assessment Authority for Wales	www.accac.org.uk/
	3. National Council for Education and Training for Wales	www.elwa.ac.uk/elwaweb/
	4. Department of Education, Northern Ireland	www.deni.gov.uk/
	5. Scottish Executive Education Department	www.scotland.gov.uk/Topics/ Education
	6. Scottish Qualifications Authority	www.sqa.org.uk/
Uruguay	Ministerio de Educación y Cultura	www.mec.gub.uy/
Venezuela	1. Ministerio de Educación, Cultura de Deportes	www.me.gov.ve/
	2. Consejo Nacional de Universidades	www.cnu.gov.ve/
Vietnam	Ministry of Education and Training	www.edu.net.vn/
Yemen	Ministry of Education	www.yemen.gov.ye/egov/ education-english/
Zimbabwe	Ministry of Higher and Tertiary Education	www.mhet.ac.zw/index.html

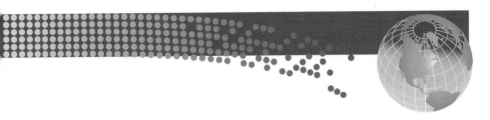

Authors

Mary Baxton
California State University Northridge

Cheryl Darrup-Boychuck
USjournal.com, LLC

Negar Davis
The Pennsylvania State University

Stephen C. Dunnett
University at Buffalo–The State
University of New York

John F. Eriksen
Bryant University

Chris J. Foley
Indiana University–Purdue
University Indianapolis

S. Kelly Franklin
University of North Carolina at Charlotte

Louis Gecenok
San Jose State University

Marjory Gooding
California Institute of Technology

Linda Heaney
Consultant in International Education

Peggy Hendrickson
University of North Texas

Linda Jahn
International Academic Credential
Evaluators, Inc.

Tracy Kaan
University of North Texas

Theodore McKown II
Kent State University

Aleka Myre
University of North Texas

June Noronha
The Bush Foundation

Panetha Theodosia Nychis Ott
Brown University

Sonja Phongsavanh
Rochester Institute of Technology

Peggy J. Printz
Study in the USA

Liz Reisberg
Boston College

Steven L. Shaw
University at Buffalo–The State
University of New York

Marjorie S. Smith
University of Denver

Rebecca Smith-Murdock
University of North Texas

Eddie West
Ohlone College

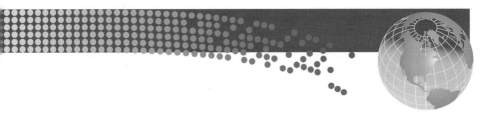

community colleges *(continued)*
  outreach to parents, 159
  power of partnerships for, 157–59
  recruitment strategies, 156–57
complexity science, 103–04
consortia
  community colleges and, 159
  familiarization (fam) tours organized
    by, 151–52
  third-party agents and, 134
consultants, educational, 7, 133, 173, 175.
    See also third-party agents
corporations, international, M.B.A. programs
    and, 172–73
Council for Higher Education
  Accreditation, 50
Council of Graduate Schools (CGS), x,
    4–5, 164, 179
Council of International Schools (CIS), ix–x
course placement, recruitment issues
    regarding, 23
credentials, foreign
  accreditation vs. recognition for, 50–51
  country files, 54
  country-specific and multicountry printed
    resources, 52–53
  credential evaluation companies, 56
  databases and listservs, 53
  determining authenticity of, 48–49
  general and multicountry printed
    resources, 52
  grading systems, 51
  media resources, 54
  one-way mailing lists/newsletters, 54
  OSEAS advisers as resources on, 55
  research on, 55–56
  U.S. benchmarks for, 47–48
  workshop materials, 55
Critical Fields List (CFL), 162
Curricular Practical Training (CPT), 155

D

databases, as foreign credentials
    resources, 53
deans, graduate school, recruitment efforts
    of, x
Denmark, increasing international student
    enrollments in, viii
departments, graduate program, recruiting
    process and, 167
dependents, recruitment issues and needs
    of, 25

Designated School Official or Responsible
    Officer, 62, 155
Destination Indiana, 159
development goals, alumni involvement in
    international recruiting and, 121
directories
  advertising in, 70, 72
  International Student Handbook, 179
  DS 2019 (immigration regulation document),
    61–62

E

Eastern Europe, Asian currency crisis and
    recruitment from, 8
The Economist, viii
economy, global, 162–63, 173–74
Education and Training Export Consortium
    (ETEC), California, 159
educational consultants, 7, 133, 173, 175.
    See also third-party agents
EducationUSA
  graduate recruiting and, 169
  M.B.A. program recruiting and, 175
  networking with offices of, 128–29, 131
  OSEAS advisers of, 55
  overseas college fair calendars of, 88
  overseas recruitment fairs and, 87
elementary education, U.S., benchmark
    credentials in, 47
English, degree programs taught in, in non-
    English-speaking countries, ix, 9,
    164, 171
English as a Second Language (ESL)
    programs, 21. *See also* Intensive
    English Programs
English language admission requirements,
    community colleges and, 154, 157
enrollment management offices, 7, 10
environmental scan, for strategic plans, 29
ethics in international student recruitment
    challenges to, 12–13
  M.B.A. admissions consultants and, 175
  NAFSA's role in, 11–12
  proactive and professional international
    admissions office, 13–14
  professional admissions officers, 14–15
  third-party agents and, 133, 137
  Wingspread Colloquium (1980) and, 4–5
Eurasia, Asian currency crisis and
    recruitment from, 8

Europe
  group tours of, 5–6, 77
  international graduate students from, 164
  M.B.A. programs in, 172, 174
  recruitment fairs in, 79
  sponsored student programs in, 94
European Council of International Schools
    (ECIS), 5–6, 128, 132, 180
evaluation
  calculating recruitment costs, 105
  as complexity science, 103–05
  market research, 107–08
  precision marketing, 108
  of prospective students by alumni, 124
  quality vs. quantity of inquiries, 106–07
  return on investment case studies, 105–06
  of strategic plan, 35
E-Verify program, 163
Exchange Visitor Program, 62
expenditures. *See also* budgets; return on
    investment
  identification of, for strategic plan, 34
external assessment, for strategic
    plans, 30–31

F

"F-1 for Beginners" (NAFSA workshop), 63
F-1 visas, for students, 60, 61, 162
Facebook, 73
faculty
  annual recruitment plan and, 42
  at community colleges, 154
  education abroad programs and, x
  graduate recruiting and, 166–67, 168, 169
fairs, recruitment. *See* recruitment fairs
familiarization (fam) tours, 151–52
Federation of English Language and
    Consulting Association (FELCA), 151
fees, for visas, 58, 59
financial aid, ix, xi, 13, 20, 124
Foreign Student Recruitment: Realities and
    Recommendations (Wingspread
    Colloquium, 1980), 4–5
for-profit companies, 7. *See also* third-
    party agents
France
  competition for international students
    and, 8
  international students in, ix
  M.B.A. programs in, 172
  9/11 attacks and international enrollment
    in, 9

France *(continued)*
  three-year bachelor's degrees and
    Bologna Process in, 164
  friends of alumni, M.B.A. program recruiting
    and, 174
Fulbright Commission, 79, 169
Fulbright Program, 93, 131

G

Germany
  competition for international students
    and, 8
  increasing international student
    enrollments in, viii
  international students in, ix
  9/11 attacks and international enrollment
    in, 9
  three-year bachelor's degrees and
    Bologna Process in, 164
goals
  for annual recruitment plan, 41
  strategic, coordinating annual recruitment
    plan with, 44–45
  strategic planning and, 33
grading systems, 51
Graduate Management Admissions Council
    (GMAC), 176, 180
Graduate Management Admissions Test
    (GMAT), 175
graduate programs
  activities and tips for success in, 168–70
  analyzing where to recruit for, 164–66
  Bologna Process and, 164
  centralized model of recruiting for, 166
  decentralized model of recruiting
    for, 166–67
  global economy and, 162–63
  international students in, 161–62
  mixed model of recruiting for, 167–68
  as planned and managed activity, 170
  September 11, 2001 terrorist attacks
    and, 162
Graduate Record Examination (GRE) Search
    Service, 168–69
grants. *See* financial aid
green cards, information about, 62
group tours
  advantages and disadvantages of, 82
  to Asia and Europe in 1970s and
    1980s, 5–6
  as first overseas recruitment trip, 76

spending per student, for international students in U.S., ix

sponsored students
  academic support services for, 98–99
  accounting system issues for, 96
  building relationships with agencies for, 99–100
  funding sources for, 93
  nonacademic services for, 97–98
  support services for, 95
  tracking, management, and reporting systems for, 97
  trends in, 93–95

STEEP (sociological/cultural, technological, economic, environment, and political environments) scanning, for strategic plans, 29

strategic plans
  action plan for, 34
  annual recruitment plan and, 40–41
  assessing success, 35
  coordinating annual recruitment plan with, 44–45
  development of mission and goals for, 32–33
  environmental scan for, 29
  examples, for international recruitment, 36–37
  external assessment and analysis for, 30–31
  as framework for international admissions, 28
  identification of key performance indicators, 33
  identification of resources, needs, and expenditures, 34
  internal assessment and analysis for, 29–30
  objectives in, 33–34
  reasons for, 27–28
  SWOT/TOWS analysis, 31–32
  travel as element in, 75–76

Student and Exchange Visitor Information Service (SEVIS), 58–59, 61, 62, 162

Student and Exchange Visitor Program (SEVP), 155

students. *See* international students

Study Illinois, 159

Study Oregon, 159

Study Washington, 159

Study Wisconsin, 159

SWOT (strengths, weaknesses, opportunities, and threats) analysis, for strategic plans, 31–32

T

teaching, as faculty focus at community colleges, 154

Technology Alert List (TAL), 162

thank you, for alumni volunteers, 125

third-party agents
  activities by, in annual recruitment plan, 42
  advantages of, 134–35
  calculating return on investment cost of, 106
  compensating, 140–41
  contracting with, 139–41
  disadvantages of, 135
  educational consultants vs., 133
  ethics in international student recruiting by, 13
  for IEPs, 151–52
  managing a relationship with, 137–39
  relationships and networks with, 131
  reliable, criteria in search for, 135–37
  scope of authority, 136
  success with, 141
  use of by U.S. colleges and universities, 4–5

three-year rule, for recruitment fairs, 150

Thunderbird School of Global Management, 171

TOEFL (Test of English as a Foreign Language), 129, 154, 175

tours. *See* group tours; travel

TOWS (threats, opportunities, weaknesses, and strengths) analysis, for strategic plans, 31–32

tracking systems, for sponsored students, 97

Transfer Credit Practices of Designated Educational Institutions (AACRAO), 50

transfers from community colleges to four-year universities, 10, 154, 157. *See also* credentials, foreign

translation
  of marketing materials, 69–70, 71, 148–49
  at overseas recruitment fairs, 87
  for Web sites, 73

travel
advertising costs vs. costs for, 67
as annual recruitment plan activity, 41,
42, 75–76
calculating return on investment cost of,
105–06
costs, 81
follow-up, 81–82
and graduate recruiting, 169
group tours, 76, 82
identifying recruiter for, 76
individual and blended, 78–80, 83
M.B.A. program recruiting and, 176
scheduling, 80–81
tour selection, 77–78
tuition
self-funded international students and
increases in, 3–4, 6, 7
at U.S. community colleges, 153,
155–56, 156
Turkey, Asian currency crisis and
recruitment from, 8
Twitter, 73
2 + 2 transfer programs, 10, 154, 157
two-year school model, familiarity of
international students with, 155

U

United Kingdom
competition for international students
and, x, 8
international students and skilled worker
policy in, 163
international students in, ix
M.B.A. programs in, 172, 174
9/11 attacks and international enrollment
in, 9
on-the-spot admission offers by, 13
United States
as destination for M.B.A. programs, 172
government funding for promoting U.S.
universities abroad by, x
international recruiting and government
agencies of, 128–31
international students in, ix
visas for sponsored students from Iraq
to, 94–95

U.S. colleges and universities. *See also*
community colleges; history of U.S.
international student recruitment
benchmark credentials in, 47–48
community college partnering with,
157–59, 160
consortia of, third-party agents and, 134
differences between IEPs and, 145–47
enrollment management offices, 7
Intensive English Programs at, 147–48
international recruitment trends in, vii
marketing M.B.A. programs separately
from, 172–73
overseas recruiting by, ix–x
quality and quantity of, ix
Web sites of organizations focused
on, 180–81
U.S. Commercial Service, 129, 130, 131, 181
U.S. Department of Commerce, U.S.
Commercial Service, 130
U.S. Department of Homeland Security
(DHS), 57, 59
U.S. Department of State
Bureau of Educational and Cultural
Affairs, 62, 129, 181
colleges and universities as resources
for, 132
Exchange Visitor Program of, 62
Office of Overseas Schools, 127
overseas recruitment fairs and, 87
visa procedures after Sept. 11 attacks,
8, 57
U.S. Foreign Service, 130–31

V

visa, definition and characteristics of, 61
visa procedures
after September 11 terrorist attacks, 8, 57
answers to immediate questions, 58
basic assumptions in immigration
law, 60–61
helpful terminology, 61–62
international students in U.S. and, vii
NAFSA immigration resources, 63
realistic, transparent, and workable, xi
for sponsored students from Iraq, 94–95
steps for international students, 59

W

Wanamaker, John, 103, 108
Washington (state), consortia-based
  international student recruitment
  efforts in, 159
Web sites. *See also* social networking sites
  advertising elements in, 70–72
  advertising using, 181
  alumni admissions counselors listed
    on, 121
  alumni video presentations for, 124
  cyber recruitment resources, 181
  graduate recruiting using, 169
  for IEP program marketing, 149
  link to EducationUSA on, 129
  overseas college fair calendars on, 87–88

Web sites *(continued)*
  pay-per-click campaigns, 108, 181
  tracking visits to, 107–08
  translated materials in HTML vs. PDF
    formats, 70
  U.S. higher education and individual
    educational institutions, 180–81
Wingspread Colloquium (1980), 4–5
Wisconsin, consortia-based international
  student recruitment efforts in, 159
Working Toward Strategic Change (1997), 27

Y

YouTube, 73